THE TEACHING FOR SOCI

William Ayers—*Series Editor*   Therese

MW00986200

Rise for Racial Justice

How to Talk About Race With Schools and Communities

**Colette N. Cann,
Kimberly Williams Brown,
and Meredith Madden**

with Robin Mallison Alpern,
Brett Collins,
Masumi Hayashi-Smith,
T. Gertrude Jenkins,
Nama Khalil, Sade Ojuola,
and Sarah Moss Yanuck

Foreword by David Stovall
Afterword by Rita Kohli

TEACHERS COLLEGE PRESS

TEACHERS COLLEGE | COLUMBIA UNIVERSITY
NEW YORK AND LONDON

Published by Teachers College Press,® 1234 Amsterdam Avenue, New York, NY 10027

Copyright © 2022 by Teachers College, Columbia University

Cover design by Miguel A. Huidor. Photograph by Glodi Miessi via Unsplash.

Library of Congress Cataloging-in-Publication Data is available at loc.gov

ISBN 978-0-8077-6714-6 (paper)
ISBN 978-0-8077-6715-3 (hardcover)
ISBN 978-0-8077-8112-8 (ebook)

Printed on acid-free paper
Manufactured in the United States of America

Contents

Foreword

The Public and the Personal Are Both Political

I am deeply humbled by the request to offer a set of meditations on the current moment in K–12 schools and the need for a public pedagogy. As a critical race theorist, I have become used to being uninvited to anything that has to do with K–12 schools or any work deemed adjacent to them. Simultaneously, this moment of racial upheaval and manufactured culture wars has been prophesized by many, but it always feels different when you're actually in the moment that you've been waiting for. The weight of the situation can hit you in a way that calls up frustration, surprise, and disillusionment. Because America hides behind an illusion of liberty while refusing its genesis in slavery, genocide, and settler colonialism, people are "shocked" when this is the topic of conversation. At the same time, many of us remain frustrated at the idea that the aforementioned realities are so overwhelming when we dare to discuss them in places supposedly centered in education. I didn't have the world-shattering experience (like some white folks had in the summer of 2020) of knowing that the majority of things they've come to claim are usually not the result of hard work or a meritocratic society. But if we are real with ourselves, it remains ridiculous and absurd to run from the realities of white supremacy/racism historically and in relation to the current moment.

Historian and community activist Dr. Timuel Black (1918–2021) would remind many of us in Chicago that *all life is political*. Not in the sense that it is some machination of a partisan ploy to shift public sentiment, but instead a reminder that all life is connected to how we understand power: the ability to build it, shift it, or capitulate to it. There is no space in our lives, publicly or personally, that is absent of these realities. Every day is an intimate political exercise in survival, refusal, acquiescence, or self-determination. If the decision is made to shift and/or build power, there must always be an inward-facing understanding (personal) and the outward-facing work (public) with others to confront any oppressive forces that move to kill the ability to organize, strategize, and build. Racial justice work with K–12 educators finds itself on this continuum.

The authors have decided to document the process of recognizing the need to place a particular indictment on the U.S. schooling system. Because it was never intended to educate *anyone,* we are often forced to find spaces external to K–12 schools to do our justice work with intention and fidelity. The good teachers we may have experienced in traditional schools did not do their radical work *because* of a system, but largely *in spite* of it. Paying homage to their work, we must always remember the indictment is never an empty accusation, but one that rests in a host of contradictions and uncomfortable realities. Because racial justice work is one that moves us away from schooling (order, compliance, and rewards for the regurgitation of the rules of white supremacy) and into education (the capacity to learn and work with others to change your condition), it is imperative that we always turn to the radical roots of struggle for our sustenance. It is the type of public-facing work that will require us to first ask deep personal questions of ourselves, including who we are and what we are willing to do in the face of those willing to maim and dismember our struggle.

This book does not run from the tensions of racial justice work in education. It is not intended to serve as a babysitting manual for those who "aren't there yet." Instead, I read the contributor's words as ones that state *if you aren't there yet, then you better get right and build with others to get there—your excuses will not absolve you!* I appreciate this tone, given the fact that this is not the time for people to "catch up." Instead, it is a moment to understand that the opposition has situated itself in a disinformation campaign aimed at dislodging the necessity of racial justice work in a country and school system that feels more comfortable with its dedication to myth and mendacity. "Free speech" has shifted to the right to lie and deceive. Racial justice has been equated to a takeover ploy orchestrated by pedophiles and aliens. The opponents of critical race theory (CRT) don't read CRT, have never read CRT, and have no plans to read CRT. As the absurdity grows by the second, we must expect the ridiculousness while working with others to state clearly what it is we are trying to do while strengthening our commitment to do it. The small group of naysayers with their massive financial coffers and media megaphones will be exposed for who they are if we dedicate ourselves to stating the terms and conditions of justice first, instead of constantly being scapegoated and backtracked into reacting to their every whim. This book is the reminder that now is not the time to panic. Instead, we can receive and overstand it as a moment that calls up the long and overdue reminder of what we are in and what we need to do.

In the end, I hope my simple offering reflects the respect and gratitude I have for the work of Drs. Cann, Williams Brown, Madden, and Rise for Racial Justice. It is the type of public pedagogy needed when many refuse to be brave as white supremacy offers its worst. I hope that if you have chosen to read their book, you will make the conscious and necessary decision to join the fight.

—David Stovall, PhD
Chicago, Illinois

Acknowledgments

COLETTE

My great grandmother, Our Own Hardy, was a one-room schoolteacher who, legend has it, never missed a day of school and crossed rushing rivers to make it to class on time. I've coached or taught young people formally as part of an institution since I was 14 years old when I started my first job as a camp counselor. I took my first official classroom teaching position in 1995 and have taught regularly since then almost every year. In all that time, following in the footsteps of my great grandmother Hardy, I only missed one class session, to attend the services of my grandmother.

My grandmother, Dorothy Cox Cann, whose name my daughter carries, left home at the age of 14 and made her way through college to become a New York City schoolteacher many years after the war. She taught and tutored math (and I followed in her footsteps, teaching high school math myself before going to graduate school). In many ways, she was one of my first teachers and I am still learning from her these many years after she passed away.

My grandfather, who passed away in 2021 at 106 years of age, was also an educator, working in New York City schools as an assistant principal for decades. Known for his photographic memory and brilliance through K–12 and college, his academic career came to a halt when he was denied admission to a historically white medical school; insulted by the expected but still surprising racism, he joined the military, where he met my grandmother. His brother and sister-in-law, by the way, were also classroom teachers. While I never had the privilege of being a student in any of their classrooms, I was certainly a student of theirs, too.

On my mother's side of the family, both of my grandparents formally had an elementary-level education, but, of course, were teachers outside the schooling system. My grandmother made sure every one of her children not only graduated college, but graduated from law school, medical school, business school, or got an architectural degree. Though I didn't know her well, I knew of her passion for her children's education.

My grandfather was a master craftsman who built the home in which my mother grew up and simultaneously held down many jobs (such as setting pins in the local bowling alley before it became automated) to make sure his family's needs were met. He taught me to use almost every tool in the toolbox, together building birdhouses and windmills with exquisite craftsmanship. I learned from him to live my life with joy because, despite the obstacles that racism puts in my way, I get to choose joy—no one else. And I learned how to say with absolute honesty and sincerity to each person with whom I shared space "You are my favorite person in the world" and have it be true every single time.

I offer this acknowledgement of and dedication to my great grandmother and my grandparents—educators who were critically important to what, how, and why my sister and I teach. Teaching is both an honored inheritance and a responsibility. May Salihah, Jai, Roshan, and Asha inherit a love for teaching and wear this responsibility well.

Teaching, in our family and in Black communities, has always been about the liberation of Black people, about the abolition of limits and the pursuit of freedom dreams (Kelley, 2002), about the search for an "Afrolantica Awakening" (Bell, 1992, p. 46), about writing visionary fiction into reality (Imarisha & brown, 2015). It becomes, I believe, a revolutionary act in the classrooms of Black educators and in the homes of Black parenting adults. So, while this book will reference educational theory to explain our pedagogy, the reference to theory is a collection of fancy words to describe what Black educators and parenting adults do daily when they show up for Black students. My pedagogy is rooted in the activism of public scholars like Septima Clark and Derrick Bell and bell hooks as well as the work of my great grandmother, grandmothers, grandfathers, great aunt, and great uncle—Black educators who dared to use the tool of education in service to Black people.

KIMBERLY

To stand in gratitude with all who made this text possible is a daunting and overwhelming task. Where do I start? At the beginning with my parents? Or with my favorite K–12 teacher who saw me, took an interest in me, and believed in me to pursue the passions I was developing? It does not feel right to name a specific moment when it started, because the journey to this moment has been punctuated by many experiences and made possible through many people. I will name a few of them through this acknowledgement, but I do so understanding that I will not do so perfectly. I do so knowing that inevitably I will forget to name someone or to remember a moment that was pivotal in my growth. I do so nonetheless knowing how important my own epistemological journey to this moment has been and acknowledging that I have pursued this journey intellectually as well as experientially.

When I first migrated to the United States in 1999, I was not politically active, although I had a strong sense of justice and had always been someone who fought for the rights of those I thought were being treated unfairly. In fact, I was always the child who brought home or to church people I met on the street because they were struggling or otherwise not in my typical friend group. So, I was not apolitical but not yet activated through language and orientation. The beginning of my politicization took place at home where as a little girl I saw my mother fighting against patriarchal oppression through the church and my dad's staunch support of her, often to their detriment. I thank my parents for being who they are and for demonstrating in my home what it meant to advocate on behalf of myself and others. They were my first teachers in every way and for lessons that are still foundational to my core.

I used to think that my politicization also did not take place in college because as a sociology and psychology major at a small liberal arts college in West Virginia, I was not introduced to a single Theorist of Color. If I were introduced, it was so distinctly unmemorable that I have no recollection. All the knowledge producers were white men whose theories only applied to particular areas of my life. I now understand that my experience as a Black woman at a predominantly white college with very few Black students or Students of Color was the theoretical foundation I could not find in any text. What I learned from being embraced by the other Black students (although I was learning what it meant to be Black because I had not been racialized Black prior to then) has been ineffable until now. I specifically want to name Katrina Nasiru, who passed away from cancer in 2021, and Kyra Lloyd, who led our all-Black STEP team and insisted we perform everywhere and for every event on that campus. Blackness was not only visible but political on our campus because of them and women like them. I thank them for the role they played in my politicization.

They taught me how to be in solidarity with other Black students, mostly women, and how to navigate the contradictions on a predominantly white West Virginia campus.

Feminist theory and intergroup dialogue (IGD) cemented my intellectual politicization. The moments before feminist theory and intergroup dialogue were experiential and provided context I was not yet able to name. I thank all my teachers who were patient as I worked the intellectual muscle that allowed me any access to critical thinking. Specifically, I thank Linda Carty, who beyond caring deeply about my intellectual growth, cared deeply about my growth as a person, mother-scholar, and academic. She pushed me, supported me, and held me like Black mothers—blood and otherwise—do. I thank Chandra Mohanty, whose third-world politics provided an intellectual roadmap I did not know was possible. I laid at her feet (and still do) as she pushed us to be critical thinkers and better feminists. I thank Marcelle Haddix and Dalia Rodriguez, who saw the work, saw me, and held me when I needed it most. I thank Gretchen Lopez, whose grace and poise in the face of the most difficult facilitation situations is so deeply admirable. I thank her for also pushing me intellectually while supporting my work as a mother-scholar and as a practitioner. I thank Kelsey John, Lynn Dew, Bernetta Parson, Jordan West, Julie Ficarra, Laura Jaffe, Camilla Bell, The Radikal Birds, and so many graduate students who helped my intellectual formation. I salute Fumi Showers, my comrade sister friend writing about the Black immigrant struggle from the West African context. Who knew our intellectual projects would be so closely aligned? Thank you for making my way a little easier as you blaze the trail with your brilliance and tenacity.

Most recently, I thank the teachers about whom and for whom this book is written. From them, I have learned the most about people, the complexities of antiracist work, and what my own boundaries and limits are. To create RISE for Racial Justice took much intellectual and personal stamina. They were instrumental in the forging of my own capacity to make it happen. I thank the education department at Vassar College, who values this work enough to allow me to teach it as part of the curriculum and to support the community projects as part of my scholarship. You have made doing this work in a conservative, often difficult K–12 context so much easier.

Colette and Meredith are the best collaborators I have ever worked with. The process has been smooth, and systematic as it has built deeper bonds of friendship between us. Meredith, I would not have made it through graduate school without you literally decoding what the requirements meant, showing me examples, and being frank with me about the politics of pursuing a PhD. I love that we can talk IGD in shorthand, facilitate a dialogue session, and not miss a beat as we manage the rigors of family life and other important priorities. Thank you for standing with me on this project. I cannot imagine anyone else I would choose. Colette, I owe you my professional trajectory. You not only saw my potential, but you made sure I had the tools and the support to succeed. You live mentorship, you do not only talk about its importance. I thank you for always being frank, for always decoding the politics, and for always trying to help where you can. This book would not be possible for me if you were not ok with me taking up the mantle you left behind to teach teachers in a community I was new to, making the content my own, and collaborating with me in many ways. You are one of a kind. Thank you.

Finally, thanks to my family, Ian, Zuri, and Zaire Brown, who bring more joy than I can describe. They are the real MVPs as I juggle long days and nights, much travel, and sometimes little sleep. They give me the space to work. For that I am grateful. They love me unconditionally and are always happy to see me. You make it worth it every day, and I hope my efforts to create a better world for you as you experience many classrooms in your lifetime are worth every sacrifice.

MEREDITH

One thing racial and social justice work has taught me is that if you are going to talk the talk, you have got to walk the walk. This is the work of solidarity. It is the work of action. It is the work of love. Colette, you extended the invitation to *Rise for Racial Justice* and my mind and heart have grown in tremendous ways. You have been an extraordinary guide through this process. I am so grateful to you. Kim, our journey has been long. All of those years ago learning on the path at Syracuse and now we are making another path forward in this work together. Thank you for being a partner and friend in creating just educational spaces. As scholar-activist moms, this work required showing up for one another in ways that I will always remember. Thank you, Colette and Kim, for showing up and holding up. My love and respect to you both always.

I am deeply humbled to be in this particular moment of my life where dreams I held as a young girl are being realized. First, I dreamed of being a writer. The second dream of mine was expressed in a first-grade assignment. We were asked to draw a picture of something we dreamed of with the expectation that we would draw something creative we remembered from our dreams when asleep. I remember my 6-year-old self struggling to understand what we were being called on to do and I wound up misinterpreting the assignment. I didn't draw a scene from my nighttime dreams. I drew what I dreamt about in a "hopes and dreams" kind of way. I drew a picture of myself with a text bubble above my head and wrote in crayon, "I dream about loving people." Now I didn't do the assignment "right" according to my teacher. However, my first teacher, my mother, thought it was perfect. She ended up framing that picture. And so let my acknowledgement begin right there with my mom, Linda Madden. Mom, thank you from the bottom of my heart for creating the most loving and nurturing home for me as a child. A home that gave me the most important thing that shaped my life: love. From a young age I knew that the most valuable thing I had to give others is what you had always given me: love. This is a book about racial equity and justice for educators and communities. There is no separation of love from this work. Thank you, Momma. The love that I bring to my life's work is the legacy of your mothering. Of course, the legacy of a house of love is also shared by my father, Peter Madden. Dad, from a young age you have always shown me the importance of showing up honestly as who you are wherever you are. You have also shown me what it means to stay the course. In your own way, you always called things out in the world, especially injustices. You showed that when things were problematic it is ok to have a strong opinion and to share it. You and mom sacrificed so much for me to be at the point where my dreams can be realized. Without your loyalty to me and Ronan there is simply no way I would be writing this right now. Thank you, Dad. I have tried to carry the legacy of my parent's work into my own parenting, which brings me to the person that I hold at the core of my heart, my son, Ronan. Ronan, you have always been my promise. I always have told you that I loved you before I even knew you, and it's true. And to know you is to love you even more than I thought possible. My journey through social and racial justice work has been long, and you have been there for such an important portion of that time. When I think back to all the critical conversations we had because you wanted to know what I was learning about in graduate school sometimes I am astounded. You were learning right there along side of me, coming to those sociology classes at MVCC, the social justice conference, and expressing curiosity and commitment to wanting things to be more just for other people from the youngest age. You are possibly the most empathetic person I have ever known and our conversations on racial and social justice have always inspired and sustained me. You have a gift of truly seeing and valuing people. You have the most admirable traits, which make me know that our world is so much better for having you in it. Keep making the choices you know to be true, Ronan. I am blessed among mothers to be able to bear witness to your remarkable life. I love you.

I am fortunate to have had an amazing community of people across my journey. I want to thank anyone who invested their time teaching me across every stage of my life. I want to highlight my sociology professors at Hobart and William Smith, with a particular thank you to Dr. Jack Harris for imparting on me the idea of social responsibility and social consciousness and then raising it. I want to thank Dr. Richard Mason for seeing a sophomore student's passion to disrupt social inequality and telling me "Go get your PhD and write about this!" Thank you to Dr. Dunbar Moodie for challenging me on my writing, holding me to a high standard, and not accepting anything less. And thank you to Dr. Renee Monson for opening my eyes to doing research on social issues. You all changed my life. Thank you to the amazing folks in the Cultural Foundations of Education program and Women's and Gender Studies programs at Syracuse University. To the brilliant Dr. Gretchen E. Lopez, your dedication to me as my advisor and mentor has left the biggest imprint on my mind and heart. Dr. Chandra Mohanty, thank you for teaching me and working with me in ways that gave me a new lens. I see the world so much more clearly now, and that has shaped all of the work I do for the public. Dr. Margo Okazawa-Rey, thank you for being an inspiration source and for helping me grow as a social justice educator. Thank you also to my many other friends and colleagues across the years from MVCC to Syracuse to Hamilton and Utica who have worked to make educational spaces more equitable. It's a privilege to walk alongside you.

My students inspire me every day to keep walking this walk. I'm thinking back to my students from my days teaching middle school in the Bronx, NY, to my students in Trumansburg, NY. I am holding in my heart a very special cohort of students from Hamilton College who quite literally journeyed with me across our years together. My love and respect to each of you: Angélica Ramos, Delta Reyes, Diamond Jackson, Edgar Otero, Fluffy Aguilar, Helen Stutsman, Joe Pucci, Kelli Mackey, Sacharja Cunningham, Shaina Coronel Pazmino, Syon

Powell, Aoífe Thomas, and the whole Highlander crew from *Education, Teaching and Social Change* who created the most beautiful and just classroom experience.

To all of the folks who have participated in any of my public antiracist education classes over these past years . . . you have trusted me to guide you on your journey to be antiracist students, parents, and educators, and it has been a tremendous privilege.

My friends show up in my life and uphold me in ways that enable me to do the work I do. Colleen Soden, my sister, you extend the definition of family for me and have always held me in your ultimate care. Thank you, Colly, for being a constant reminder of how beautiful the world is because you bring that beauty into the world every day. Mark Soden, you have always been clear in your love and support of me. It matters more than you know. Liam Soden (my amazing godson) and Alyse Soden (sweetest "niece"), I love you both so much. The world will be better because of you. Sara Bell, thank you for being a constant listener, encourager, and supporter of me in every single way since as far back as I can remember. Your impact is treasured. I love and thank each of these amazing people from my HWS fam: Pam Burkhalter, Jen Hurley, Becky Scheer, Amy Schubmehl, and Meredith Moriarty. Momo, you are a steady force of a friend and have helped me grow as a person for so long. Miki Alroy, you have helped me bridge my antiracist work across spaces. Thank you for always being willing to talk, motivate, and offer clear perspective. While I sifted through moments of challenge you steadily reminded me of the greater purpose: unity. Erica Shaw, thank you my dear friend for being my "process partner" in doing antiracist work. Erica, for years you have always been right there to listen, critically reflect, offer thoughtful and intentional insights and constant support. The countless conversations we have had have helped me stay the course.

Peter Madden, Nat Madden, Rachel Madden, and Anna Madden, thank you for unconditional love. Rachel and Anna, you are each incredible women and the world is abundantly better with you here. Keep dreaming and working hard. You make me so proud. Richard Hunt, thank you for being a wonderful cousin and also an important mentor on my journey.

Last, I want to acknowledge my late grandmother, Hazel Willmot, whose home was a place where I dreamed many times about being a writer and who, along with my mom, always told me that this is exactly what I could be. For her, it was always a matter of when, not if. I love you, Gramma.

ACKNOWLEDGMENTS TO THE RISE AND
TEACHERS COLLEGE PRESS TEAMS

The three of us would also like to express gratitude to the RISE family. To Penny for her administrative and course support, creative design, and for bringing to life our podcast series. To Miguel for the design of our website and all things that require a designer's touch. And to the facilitators of RISE who plan, collaborate, celebrate, teach, and hold space for critical conversations about race and schooling.

To the series editors, Bill Ayers and Therese Quinn, thank you for including our book in your fine series, *Teaching for Social Justice*. We are humbled to have our book listed among this group of brilliant texts. Thank you, Sarah Biondello, for patiently guiding, urging, and nudging us when needed and providing such spot-on advice. Thank you for your support throughout the development of this manuscript. From our proposal to print, you believed in this work and kept us focused on getting it out the door. And to Susan Liddicoat, thank you for taking such great care with our manuscript, gently making suggestions while embracing the spirit, intent, and vision of our manuscript. It was our first experience as writers to take on suggested revisions so enthusiastically. And to the rest of the team at Teachers College Press, Nancy Power, Dave Strauss, and Caritza Berlioz, thank you for your ongoing support.

REFERENCES

Bell, D. (1992). *Faces at the bottom of the well: The permanence of racism*. Basic Books.

Imarisha, W., & brown, a. m. (2015). *Octavia's brood: Science fiction stories from social justice movements*. AK Press.

Kelley, R. D. G. (2002). *Freedom dreams: The black radical imagination*. Beacon Press.

Introduction

On May 25, 2020, Derek Chauvin, a white Minneapolis police officer, kneeled on the neck of George Floyd, a Black man, long enough to kill him. For over 7 minutes, Derek Chauvin ignored the pleas of George Floyd and bystanders to allow him to breathe. After 7 minutes, George Floyd lost consciousness and died an hour later. George Floyd's murder, caught on a video that went viral, is one of many resulting from a long history of state-sanctioned violence against Black people and their communities. As of March 25, 2021, a year after the murder of George Floyd, there have been as many as 229 additional Black lives lost at the hands of police (Rahman, 2021). These murders (only some of which received public attention), racism supported by the White House, an election year that seemed intent on simultaneously naming and ignoring race, and the disproportionate effect of COVID-19 on Black communities launched a renewed call for Black lives to matter, prompting protests globally.

There was a resulting demand for antiracism workshops by individuals and companies to help the public make sense of what they witnessed in videos proliferated by online media. Organizations such as Crossroads Anti-racism Organizing and Training saw the requests for their workshops grow 10-fold, while books about race and racism written by authors such as Ibram X. Kendi, Ijeoma Oluo, and Layla Saad topped bestseller lists (Judkis, 2020). What we refer to as *public racial literacy campaigns*—educational efforts to provide antiracism training in out-of-school spaces—were waged in remote environments across the United States by organizations whose primary mission is to educate the public about race, racism, and antiracism.

UNDERSTANDING PUBLIC LITERACY CAMPAIGNS

Many of these organizations, during 2020, conducted *public racial literacy campaigns*. That is, in addition to their mission-guided work, they took strategic action to broaden their reach, increase their offerings, intensify their message, and focus their workshops to respond to the racialized, political, health, and environmental injustices of the moment. Thus, a *public racial literacy campaign* is the work that individuals (oftentimes public scholars) and organizations launch to increase the racial literacy of the youth and adult public outside of formal school settings in response to a racialized historical moment. *Public*, in this sense, borrows from the term "public pedagogy" to highlight this work as done in "spaces, sites, and languages of education and learning that exist outside of the walls of the institution of schools" (Sandlin et al., 2010, p. 1). *Racial literacy* is defined as the ability to read a racialized world—to read racialized personal, interpersonal, cultural, institutional, and structural actions and interactions in the world and to understand how race and racism play a part in intentions, processes, and outcomes (Frankenberg, 1993; Grosland & Matias, 2017; Guinier, 2006; Twine, 2004). It is, as Guinier (2006) argued, to make racism visible. Guinier defined *racial literacy* as "the capacity to decipher the durable racial grammar that structures racialized hierarchies and frames the narrative of our republic" (p. 100).

For the past 25 years increasing the racial literacy of youth and adults has been a focus in some schooling spaces (Derman-Sparks & Ramsey, 2011; hooks, 1994; Okun, 2010; Tatum, 1997/2017). Less well documented, though extensive in its reach and history, is this work in out-of-school spaces—work by organizations such as the People's Institute for Survival and Beyond, Othering and Belonging, and Race Forward. This book seeks to highlight the work of one such organization, RISE for Racial Justice, which launched a *public racial literacy campaign* in 2020, when the nation's interest in learning about and exploring the history and present reality of racism was at a high; the protests following the murder of George Floyd focused the public's attention on anti-Black racism, and the desire to make sense of that political moment and calls for racial justice increased. In fact, if the plethora of company statements publicizing a commitment to Black lives is any indication, the desire for more racial literacy training converged with the interests of corporate America to be seen as antiracist (Harper, 2020; Mull, 2020).

RISE for Racial Justice represents our collaboration as three public scholars at three different college campuses to offer racial literacy courses to K–12 teachers, parenting adults, and youth. Started in spring 2017 in response to mounting tensions between the predominantly Black, Indigenous, and People of Color (BIPOC) K–12 student population and primarily white staff in two New York school districts, RISE for Racial Justice designed and taught one introductory course on race to teachers after school. The course has been taught every semester since.

In March 2020, the course went remote due to COVID-19 restrictions on in-person gatherings. Following the murder of George Floyd, RISE for Racial Justice received over 600 requests for a course that accommodates 25 participants. Seemingly overnight, RISE for Racial Justice grew. This book offers insight into the work of RISE for Racial Justice broadly and the *public racial literacy campaign* it launched in response to an historical moment when their work intensified.

The mission of RISE for Racial Justice is to build capacity in communities where racial literacy is used and understood to be a revolutionary practice that saves the lives of BIPOC teachers and students. In our work, we often hear from Teachers of Color just how liberating the courses we offer are because, in the K–12 setting, racial literacy is not seen as vital. White teachers often remark about the importance of their own growing racial literacy to their ability to teach lovingly and effectively.

HOW THE THREE OF US ENTERED THE WORK
WITH RISE FOR RACIAL JUSTICE

The three of us entered this collaborative work that is RISE for Racial Justice through friendship. And, indeed, even the process of writing this book is made possible by that relationship among three mother-scholars committed to racial justice in and the abolition and decolonization of schooling spaces. And that friendship has been critical to doing our work with integrity; to dishonor each other by enacting white supremacist culture values while attempting to do antiracism work would be hypocritical and harmful. Instead, our work together is guided by core principles. These principles include centering racial justice in how we treat each other, creating opportunities for our continued growth, and operating at every level with as much transparency as possible. And, most important, we are guided by an ethic of care and love for each other that centers our wellness and the wellness of our loved ones as the most profound expression of justice.

Colette

My family lived in New York until I was 5. Everything I remember about New York was Black. African masks adorned the walls in our apartment. My parents wore Dashikis when we went grocery shopping. Everyone I knew was Black—my two best friends, everyone in my grandmother's neighborhood, everyone in my grandfather's neighborhood, my cousins, my aunties, my uncles. My small world was Black. And yet it was not until we moved to California and my father placed me in a predominantly (and historically) white elite elementary school that race was something that I thought about.

My memories during elementary school are brief sentences with exclamation marks at the end. The day I was called "nigger mouse" for my afropuffs, the questions about how often I washed my hair, the way my mom laughed differently when she came to school from how she laughed in the backyard playing Bid Whist with Black family friends, the history lessons about slavery in a class taught by a white teacher with a predominantly white class. Race only became salient in my life when I was one of the "onlys."

As a Black elementary school student in a predominantly white school, I experienced racial microaggressions that I did not know how to process or respond to (especially when they came from an adult). I was fortunate to be able to bring those experiences home to share with my parents, who helped me heal from these micro/macroaggressions and stave off, for as long as possible, racial battle fatigue.

When I started teaching math at a similar school years later, my focus and purpose quickly became supporting BIPOC students—helping them to survive and perhaps even thrive at a predominantly white school. After teaching for a few years, I went to graduate school, hoping to understand how to support Black youth in K–12 settings.

In graduate school, though, I had access to theory that I hadn't previously learned. Reading people like bell hooks and Audre Lorde and Michael Omi and Gloria Ladson-Billings changed my life. Their words wrapped around my K–12 experience, adding parenthetical citations to each event. I was fortunate to teach a section of a race theory course for undergraduate students under Pedro Noguera and then to coteach (and later lead a team for) a course called Current Issues in Education. In these courses, we introduced students to social and race theory and engaged them in dialogues about social and racial injustices in schooling. To these courses, I brought my love for teaching, my commitment for supporting BIPOC students, and my passion for theory. Many of the pedagogical practices that I was taught in my training for these courses are rooted in critical pedagogy and democratic education and, thus, align with intergroup dialogue practices.

In my first academic position at a small liberal arts college in New York, I used these same teaching practices to make theory accessible in courses on contemporary issues in education and critical race theory. In my 10 years at this institution, I worked with students, staff, and faculty to host dialogues about race—following in the footsteps of Ed Pittman, who hosted intergroup dialogues for many years prior; he encouraged this work, offering historical documents, his experience and his support. In fact, the first iteration of RISE for Racial Justice was a center started by students to host dialogues about race in dormitories and other out-of-classroom spaces. As their mentor, I was privileged to work closely with them. When they graduated, they asked me to continue their work.

After the 2016 presidential election, a new need for dialogue about race arose. The K–12 educators in local school districts were struggling to make sense of how race and racism played out during the election and what it meant for shifting dynamics in their classrooms and schools. I created a course on race for K–12 educators based on the types of courses that we taught undergraduates; this course used the four-levels-of-racism pedagogical framework to raise the racial literacy of participants. I partnered with a local antiracism trainer, Robin Alpern, to teach the course. RISE for Racial Justice was reborn with a new focus on direct work with K–12 educators (and later with parenting adults and youth).

Five years later, I am thrilled that this work continues with Kim and Meredith. Their experience and training in intergroup dialogue and race theory have deepened and broadened the work we are able to do. As a team of mother-scholars committed to racial justice, our partnership offers friendship, advice, collegiality, consultation, and love.

Kim

As I sit to write this in December, 2021, bell hooks has been gone for a week. This fact may seem irrelevant to my brief, partial biography, but I seem to be living my life in "before bell hooks'" (bbh) passing and "after bell hooks'" passing (abh). It is largely because I read a tribute to her that said she was a Black girl like me who had questions about her experiences. It is also because she was bell hooks and her passing has hit me hard.

I was curious long before I or anyone else could or would call me a feminist, antiracist, public scholar. I grew up in a conservative Christian home and, like hooks, was deeply disturbed by the patriarchal chain of command. My dad was a soft-spoken man who did not perpetuate much of what I now understand to be toxic masculinity, but everywhere around me men and boys dominated and terrorized. Although I had questions, it was not until after my first graduate degree that I met bell hooks on paper and her words gave me new language and new life to fully pursue the questions I had. It is no wonder then that during my time as a graduate student I sought spaces that would help me unpack the realities of my life. Women's studies, African American studies, and critical educational studies were the academic fields that had the greatest impact on me. These fields allowed me to blend feminist consciousness and politics with intergroup dialogue praxis, so I was not only theorizing about what I had experienced but experiencing and building new realities through intergroup dialogue (IGD).

My feminist IGD approach to teaching and research began to take shape in the feminist communities that nurtured my curiosity and honed my writing and research. IGD with the accountability measures through co-facilitation and full attention to *process* over product allowed me to sit with discomfort and with the things I did not yet fully understand. My graduate experience was full of revelations, processes, and language acquisition—literacy. Neither my undergraduate studies nor my first master's degree prepared me to think critically about social issues. But I had already been thinking critically about social issues and did not need the academy to validate my thinking. I often reflect on my current students who are introduced to critical theory and the nature of it is so abstract that it sends them spinning because they have no way of anchoring it through lived experiences. For myself I needed critical theory to nurture me and to anchor me in my undergraduate studies, but like so many who attend predominantly white institutions, my education was devoid of critical theory even though I was a sociology major. By the time I entered a doctoral program, I had acquired another 10 years of lived experience in the United States, and that, coupled with my experiences as a Black immigrant woman from Jamaica, provided enough anchor for all the feminist theories, critical educational theories, and African diasporic theories to give me life and new meaning. They gave me a road map for navigating the world.

I am now the founder and director of the Intergroup Dialogue Collective (IGDC) at Vassar College in Poughkeepsie, NY. The collective itself and my directorship were both a long time in the making. In 2003, the Vassar College community began engaging in the praxis of IGD through campus community dialogues sponsored by its then named Office for Diversity and Equity under the leadership of Edward Pittman. IGD is an educational model that brings together participants from multiple social-identity groups in a cooperative, small-group learning environment. It often involves members of groups with a history of conflict or limited opportunities to engage in deep and meaningful discussion of controversial, challenging, or divisive issues. The goals of IGD include the following:

- Understanding group beginnings and relationship building
- Understanding social identities and the role of social structures, power, privilege, and institutions in creating and maintaining inequality
- Developing intergroup and other communication skills
- Planning and enacting collaboration

The purpose of introducing IGD to Vassar College's campus was to foster dialogue among undergraduate students, faculty, and administrators about issues of social identity.

Although these dialogues paused for many years, a conversation between Edward Pittman and Colette Cann brought the spirit of these dialogues back into the Vassar College community. Though an IDG (intergroup dialogue) model was not used, students from the Education Department, in partnership with Colette, brought back conversations about race and gender in social spaces such as dormitories. These conversations also formalized into courses on race, racism, and antiracism in the broader K–12 community with educators. My introduction to RISE for Racial Justice was upon Colette's departure from Poughkeepsie; I continued teaching community courses for Poughkeepsie educators and parenting adults. Over time, I transitioned the courses to using an IDG model.

In spring 2018, Edward Pittman and I reintroduced formal IGDs back onto the Vassar College campus, this time teaching the first-ever curricularly approved, unit-bearing IGD course. IGD courses have been a regular part of the curriculum since that time and the team of instructors teaching these courses banded together to create a collective who began to envision IGD as a critical part of the fabric of Vassar College. We started the Intergroup Dialogue Collective, which now serves both the campus and the broader community (including the K–12 antiracism courses for educators and parenting adults).

For example, in 2020 we offered both a course to local K–12 teachers about race as well as a dialogue space about race for employees (and another for students) in response to the heightened racial tension following the murder of George Floyd. IGDC has since grown into an officially chartered nonprofit that serves the Vassar College community as well as K–12 organizations and families beyond the campus. The mission of the IGDC is to engage individuals and groups in a culture of shared meaning, community engagement, and social justice by providing opportunities to practice the skills of IGD.

Meredith

A few years ago, I participated in a workshop on community with Margo Okazawa-Rey in Clinton, NY. There was a moment when we were invited to reflect on and share our name story. "My name is Meredith (she/her)," I said, "but people who know me from childhood call me 'Mere.'" Our identities shift in many ways over time. In many ways they also stay firmly rooted. As "Mere" I was a child of curiosity, imagination, and consciousness. I wondered at the why and how of the world around me. When I learned of inequity and injustice in its many shapes and forms, I felt it physically from a young age. My heart hurt. Empathy has been a fundamental part of my racial and social justice journey.

As I worked to express myself from my younger years through young adulthood, I encountered many folks who noted my passion, especially in my writing. What I lacked and needed though was the language to name experience. I needed a critical literacy. As a white woman, I also needed consciousness raising and to grasp my positionality. I needed to be prepared with praxis—for example, the praxis of not entering in or creating antiracist spaces that reproduce or sustain harm but instead cultivate deep listening, perspective-taking, awareness-raising, community, agency, solidarity, and action.

As I journeyed through education spaces, I slowly began gathering the words and ideas to name inequity and injustice from the root up to the blooms. Being a sociology major at William Smith College was my first dip into concepts of social responsibility and critical thinking,

while the heavy lift of building a specific antiracist and feminist critical literacy happened in the Departments of Cultural Foundations of
Education, Women's and Gender Studies, and Sociology at Syracuse
University (SU). Being trained in critical dialogic pedagogy and serving as an IDG facilitator gave me space to put theory into praxis. It
was during that time that spaces were created for me and others by
antiracist and feminist faculty mentors so I and we could focus on
gaining a racial, feminist, and social justice literacy to name and to
dialogue on what inequity and injustice meant in and for the public,
and specifically within public-school education. This was personally
valuable to me because I entered graduate school after having taught
for 5 years as a public-school teacher. It was also during my time at SU
that I began to describe myself as a publicly engaged antiracist, feminist scholar activist. That is the location from which I work to this day.

From where I enter the work today is not happenstance. I enter
the work today as the legacy of the work and works of so many who
have traveled before me and alongside me. I have learned that antiracist and feminist work is process work—intentional work, a blend
of heart and mind, and also hand. This is work of action. Action is
anchored to community, criticality, and reflection. Action in which
bell hooks beckons to us is anchored in love. It is love.

In December 2019, I reflected on the ways I was engaging my
community and where there was the opportunity to create spaces
that could impact others. I knew that the social justice curriculum of
my undergraduate education studies classrooms was transformative,
based on years of student and community feedback, and I thought of
who else might benefit from gaining a literacy to better prepare them
to meet the moments of invitation for dialogues on race and education
in the United States. I knew that the people I needed to create space
for were teachers across all stages of the profession. And so, to mark
Martin Luther King Jr. Day as a day of action, I put out a call to the
public, inviting interested teachers looking to gain skills to dialogue
on race, racism, antiracism, and education to join me at a local library
that night. Teachers from multiple districts showed up and we met
across four weeks that winter. Soon after came a community education course for youth, followed by one for parents and caregivers, and
eventually school consultancies on diversity, equity, inclusion, and
justice through my program, The Equity Prof.

Broadly, The Equity Prof seeks to create equitable and just K–12
spaces by offering professional development anchored in antiracism,
IGD, and inclusivity and belonging. In conversation with one of my

graduate school colleagues, Kim Williams Brown, I learned that she and a colleague, Colette Cann, were doing similar work in their own locations. Soon after, I would connect with Kim and Colette to learn about RISE for Racial Justice. What began as a conversation turned into an invitation to make links across our work, and soon I was facilitating for RISE for Racial Justice, teaching a course for youth and a course for educators on IGD pedagogy. What has risen out of this work has been solidarity with all those in RISE, from facilitators to participants, as we have come together to move forward a racial literacy movement, not a moment. I see this book as a legacy of the solidarity of this antiracist education movement.

OVERVIEW OF THIS BOOK

We hope to offer through this book an examination of RISE for Racial Justice to provide a view of the curriculum, the pedagogical choices we make, and the moments of promise and challenge the organization and its facilitators face. At a time when there is so much interest in racial literacy courses, this book seeks to make a unique contribution to the discussion about antiracism training for K–12 educators, parenting adults, and young people in out-of-school spaces. Educational research has more frequently (though not sufficiently) looked at racial literacy efforts in schooling spaces (Vetter & Hungerford-Kressor, 2014) and in teacher education (Sealey-Ruiz, 2011; Sealey-Ruiz & Greene, 2015). Less frequently, though, has educational research turned to the study of racial literacy efforts in out-of-school spaces (Kohli et al., 2018) and with populations that include more than teachers (Love & Muhammad, 2017). This book endeavors to fill this gap by offering a view into RISE for Racial Justice and a discussion of the work that it does in out-of-schooling spaces to increase the racial literacy of educators, parenting adults, and youth.

The book has three parts, with eleven chapters in total. The two chapters in Part I provide a rationale for antiracism training for K–12 communities and a history of some organizations that offer this training. In Part II, Chapters 3–8 use the method of narrative autoethnography to illuminate the various courses offered by the facilitators of RISE for Racial Justice. In the third and final part, Chapters 9–11 share the lessons learned and explicitly discuss challenges faced in antiracism training. Prior to each part of the book, a more thorough discussion of each chapter is outlined.

REFERENCES

Derman-Sparks, L., & Ramsey, P. G. (2011). *What if all the kids are white? Anti-bias multicultural education with young children and families.* Teachers College Press.

Frankenberg, R. (1993). *White women, race matters. The social construction of whiteness.* University of Minnesota Press.

Grosland, T. J., & Matias, C. E. (2017). Fervent fortitude: Exploring emotions and racial literacy as antiracist pedagogy. *Journal of Curriculum Theorizing, 32*(2), 72–83.

Guinier, L. (2006). From racial liberalism to racial literacy: Brown v. Board of Education and the interest-divergence dilemma. *The Journal of American History, 91*(1), 92–118.

Harper, S. R. (2020, July 16). Corporations say they support Black Lives Matter. Their employees doubt them. *Washington Post.* Retrieved January 10, 2022, from https://www.washingtonpost.com/outlook/2020/06/16/corporations-say-they-support-black-lives-matter-their-employees-doubt-them.

hooks, b. (1994). *Teaching to transgress: Education as the practice of freedom.* Routledge.

Judkis, M. (2020, July 8). Anti-racism trainers were ready for this moment. Is everyone else? *Washington Post.* Retrieved January 10, 2022, from https://www.washingtonpost.com/lifestyle/style/anti-racism-trainers-were-ready-for-this-moment-is-everyone-else/2020/07/07/df2d39ea-b582-11ea-a510-55bf26485c93_story.html.

Kohli, R., Nevárez, A., & Arteaga, N. (2018). Public pedagogy for racial justice teaching: Supporting the racial literacies of Teachers of Color. The Assembly: *A Journal for Public Scholarship on Education, 1*(1), 17–27.

Love, B., & Muhammad, G. E. (2017). Critical community conversations: Cultivating the elusive dialogue about racism with parents, community members, and teachers. *The Educational Forum, 81,* 1–4.

Mull, A. (2020, June 3). Brands have nothing real to say about racism:-Corporate America is ready to take action . . . or something. *The Atlantic.*

Okun, T. (2010). *The emperor has no clothes: Teaching about race and racism to people who don't want to know.* Information Age Publishing.

Rahman, K. (2021, May 25). Full list of 229 people killed by police since George Floyd murder. *Newsweek.* Retrieved January 10, 2022, from https://www.newsweek.com/full-list-229-black-people-killed-police-since-george-floyds-murder-1594477.

Sandlin, J. A., Schultz, B. D., & Burdick, J. (2010). Understanding, mapping, and exploring the terrain of public pedagogy. In J. A. Sandlin, B. D. Schultz, & J. Burdick (Eds.), *Handbook of public pedagogy: Education and learning beyond schooling* (pp. 1–6). Routledge.

Sealey-Ruiz, Y. (2011). Dismantling the school-to-prison pipeline through racial literacy development in teacher education. *Journal of Curriculum and Pedagogy, 8*(2), 116–120.

Sealey-Ruiz, Y., & Greene, P. (2015). Popular visual images and the (mis) reading of Black male youth: A case for racial literacy in urban preservice teacher education. *Teaching Education, 26*(1), 55–76.

Tatum, B. D. (1997/2017). *Why are all the Black kids sitting together in the cafeteria? And other conversations about race.* Basic Books.

Twine, F. W. (2004). A white side of black Britain: The concept of racial literacy. *Ethnic and Racial Studies, 27*(6), 878–907.

Vetter, A., & Hungerford-Kressor, H. (2014). We gotta change first: Racial literacy in a high school English classroom. *Journal of Language and Literacy Education, 10*(1), 82–99.

Part I

FOUNDATIONS FOR ANTIRACISM TRAINING

This opening part of the book consists of two chapters. In Chapter 1, two Black K–12 educators offer narratives that serve as our *why* for this book. They review the literature on the effects of racism in schools on Black students and Black teachers and offer their own observations and experiences of racism at the K–12 level. Their stories offer a compelling reason for why RISE for Racial Justice seeks as its primary mission to increase the racial literacy of educators, parenting adults, and youth. Chapter 2 then turns to an overview of organizations and published self-guided curricula that share this mission. RISE for Racial Justice grew out of and is rooted in the foundation created by these organizations and practitioners, and this chapter seeks to highlight and celebrate this longer history of antiracism training.

CHAPTER 1

The Harm to Black Educators and Black Students

A Call for Racial Literacy

T. Gertrude Jenkins and Sade Ojuola

In this chapter, we focus on the lived experiences of Black students and educators in K–12 institutions. We begin by unpacking the synchronized mechanisms of white fragility (DiAngelo, 2018) and racial battle fatigue (Acuff, 2018; Smith et al., 2006) to expose the complex intersections of being Black and being in schooling institutions. We also use the concept of interest convergence (Bell, 1980) as a lens through which to examine the complex racialized experiences of Black students and educators. Then we share our own narratives—our counterstories to dominant narratives of Black students and teachers—to humanize us and our experiences and to reveal the complexity of Black student and teacher identities and the ways they are harmed by, respond to, and heal from messages of anti-Blackness in schools.

With this chapter we seek to validate and amplify the complex experiences of Black students whose sense of personal identity and belonging are often misaligned with the dominant white supremacist culture of their school, requiring them to devise their own strategies to thrive and survive. This chapter is also written as an homage to Black educators who have often felt the stifling of their pride, potential, pedagogy, and praxis under the microscope of the white gaze (see, e.g., the work of Jay, 2009, a qualitative study of Black teachers and their experiences of race and racism in middle and high schools).

FACTORS AFFECTING RACIALIZED EXPERIENCES
OF BLACK STUDENTS AND EDUCATORS

To provide a foundation for our discussions in this chapter, we first want to unpack whiteness and the form and function of systematized white supremacy. Leonardo (2004) discusses the concepts of whiteness and white privilege not as representative of individual white people but as a global construct that serves to subjugate, exploit, and oppress. Whiteness is a constructed falsehood that collapses in its own irony, despite its historical power. The existence of a white racial identity, then, is a paradox; white people exist even as whiteness has no meaning other than to obstruct the humanity of the "others" that whiteness creates. For whiteness as a system to be successfully maintained, it requires white people to deny their own racial existence, to tacitly agree to not see the ways that white supremacy enacts racial violence by creating the "other." When pressed to see that which their survival requires they avoid seeing, white people can exhibit what Robin DiAngelo refers to as "white fragility."

White Fragility

When we look at whiteness as a mechanized system of white survival and thrival-hood, it becomes easier to understand why, when pressed, white people display symptoms of white emotionality and fragility. In her work on white fragility, DiAngelo (2011) shares the factors that cause white fragility and describes its manifestations. The six factors that contribute to white people's inability to discuss issues related to race and racism include the following:

1. Their tendency to live among themselves ("segregation")
2. Their belief in meritocracy ("universalism & individualism")
3. Their entitlement to racial comfort and the tendency to self-define as the supreme conveyors and holders of knowledge ("racial arrogance")
4. Their insistence on being accepted in all settings ("racial belonging")
5. Their ability to be free from mental bombardment around racial issues ("psychic freedom")
6. The fact that they enjoy a ubiquitous confirmation of value

DiAngelo suggests that if white people don't build up the stamina to confront the truths of systematized racism, the status quo will stay intact. In the context of the U.S. educational system, considering that over 80% of the teaching force is white (Ingersoll, et al., 2021), DiAngelo's call for a vigilance in confronting these truths is even more important because of the duplicitous ways white fragility can manifest to blame Black youth and educators for the effects of white supremacy and racism in the classroom.

According to Dumas (2016), systemized white supremacy has anti-Blackness at its core. The inferior treatment of Black children (and teachers) in schools is directly related to the still-ingrained notion that Black is equivalent to "enslaved." Because of this, educational policy, institutions, practices, and white teachers themselves manifest ill sentiments against Black bodies in ways that exacerbate anti-Blackness. Dumas posits that before any work can be done to advance educational equity, white people must grapple with existing codes and practices of anti-Blackness that are still very much alive today.

In a study on pre-service white teachers, Viesca et al. (2014) find that even when white teachers believe in and practice social justice education, their fragility blocks them from moving beyond feelings of guilt and resistance. The authors argue that simply acknowledging white privilege will not suffice; white teachers must move beyond reluctant acceptance and dig into work that identifies and removes the systems that make such privileges possible. This research is in line with other studies that have explored the deleterious effects on schooling at the hands of white teacher allies who refuse to move beyond performative gestures of racial equity in schools (Hines, 2016; Matias et al., 2016; Matias & Zembylas, 2014; Srivastava, 2005; Yoon, 2012).

Racial Battle Fatigue

Introduced by noted scholar William Smith, racial battle fatigue (RBF) is an emotional response that persons from BIPOC communities endure as a result of consistent exposure to racial microaggressions. The effects of RBF manifest emotionally and physically, from depression to high blood pressure (Smith, 2004). While further studies unpack the mechanisms of RBF to determine how it manifests phenomenologically in higher education (Smith, 2008)—in the lives of Black male college students (Smith et al., 2011) and Black womxn faculty in historically white institutions (Chancellor, 2019)—limited research exists with respect to the specific experience of Black students and teachers in K–12 institutions. In this section, we review the literature on Black student and teacher experiences of RBF.

Although the literature on Black students and their experiences with RBF is concentrated in higher education, we know that Black students experience racial micro/macroaggressions in K–12 institutions. Recently, researcher Hasan Hamilton (n.d.) has begun discussing the stresses and manifestations of these stresses among Black youth. She refers to RBF experiences by Black youth as "racial classroom and school fatigue" (RCSF):

> School-Based Racial Battle Fatigue is a form of trauma that describes the psychological, physiological, and in the case of students, behavioral symptoms where children and youth of African descent encounter racially inequitable treatment. Whether it's in the form of constant microaggressions, explicit or implicit bias, or blatant racism at the hands of adults, students oftentimes react in ways that can lead educators to label them as "angry," "confrontational" or "defiant."

The author explains that "without restorative intervention," such experiences with S-RBF "can drastically impact student's health or lead to painfully tragic results"; the impact of repeated micro/macroaggressions on Black youth deserves in-depth study.

In 2019, the American Academy of Pediatrics released a statement on the effects of racism on the wellness of young people (Trent, Dooley & Dougé, 2019). While not focused specifically on Black youth, the statement clearly shows how exposure to racism has adverse effects on the health of young children: "Although progress has been made toward racial equality and equity, the evidence to support the continued negative impact of racism on health and well-being through implicit and explicit biases, institutional structures, and interpersonal relationships is clear" (ibid., p.1).

Increased exposure to racism—whether internalized, interpersonal, institutional, or structural—as noted by scholars such as Chester Pierce and William Smith, leads to stress that can affect the well-being of Black people. The American Academy of Pediatrics (2019) notes that "the biological mechanism that emerges from chronic stress leads to increased and prolonged levels of exposure to stress hormones and oxidative stress at the cellular level. Prolonged exposure to stress hormones, such as cortisol, leads to inflammatory reactions that predispose individuals to chronic disease" Trent, Dooley & Dougé (2019, p. 2). Such prolonged exposure occurs, in part, in schools as Black youth are underestimated in their abilities, treated in racist ways informed by stereotypes of Black youth, and pigeon-holed into certain roles (see, for example, Ferguson, 2000/2020).

Most of the existing RBF literature on the stresses experienced by Black teachers focuses on their efforts to support their Black students. Existing scholarship about the experiences of Black educators broadly examines the ways in which RBF is challenged and confronted by Black educators (Acuff, 2018; Okello et al., 2020; Smith et al., 2011). Several researchers argue that the ability to lean into one's Blackness can be a mechanism for coping with RBF. By unapologetically allowing our cultural identities to manifest in our curriculum and pedagogy, instead of attempting to make meaning of the racial "cray cray" we experience (Matias & DiAngelo, 2013), we can deflect the ill and unintended micro/macroaggressive commentary and actions of our white colleagues.

Pizarro and Kohli (2018) write about the experiences of BIPOC educators with RBF in their article "I Stopped Sleeping: Teachers of Color and the Impact of Racial Battle Fatigue." This article opens with the story of one veteran Black teacher narrating her counter-story about working with a predominantly white teaching staff. The teacher, Ms. Shakur, highlights the ways that Black educators (and their students) are perceived and treated by their white colleagues. "Misread and mistrusted, Ms. Shakur constantly found that her peers thought she needed to be watched and handled, rather than seen as an in-control professional" (p. 968). As BIPOC teachers work tirelessly to create environments that honor and respect Youth of Color (despite systems in place that decentered and dishonored them), these educators experience "constant racism, racial stress, and racial battle fatigue [that is] devastating to their minds, bodies, and spirits" (Kohli, 2021, p. 84). Looking at the experiences of BIPOC K–12 teachers and their experiences with RBF, Kohli writes, "While Teachers of Color are navigating the professional stresses that all teachers are experiencing—such as deprofessionalized wages, outdated technology, and large class sizes—they are simultaneously enduring racial stress that can compromise their health and well-being" (p. 63).

Jay (2009) looks at the experiences of five Black middle and high school educators specifically and confirms that their experiences in schools mirrors the experiences of Black people in other professions; that is, they, too, experience the "dozen demons" that mar their days. One of the dozen demons experienced by educators in her study is pigeon-holing into particular roles deemed relevant to their racial identity, over-surveilled and yet ignored and overlooked. Jay also identifies new themes such as feeling "hyper-visible in one moment, yet invisible in the next" (p. 676); Black teachers were often the "only" in staff meetings and so were acutely aware of their race. However, they were also overlooked and ignored by their colleagues. Jay writes, "Ultimately, People of Color can be assaulted by so many racial microaggressions that they become both literally and figuratively tired. . . . [Their constant experiences with the dozen demons, for example,] serve to deplete not only African American educators' physical energy, but for some, their aspirations as well" (p. 680).

The Hechinger Report (Barmore, 2021) brought increased attention to the RBF experienced by Black teachers during a "year like no other," as Black teachers navigated multiple (ongoing) pandemics. In their efforts to support Black students through the COVID-19 pandemic and through the proliferation of images of state-sponsored murder of Black people on social media, they often are too depleted to support their own emotional and physical wellness. As the United States grappled with centuries-old racism in high relief and as that racism continued to spill over into their classrooms, hallways, and meetings, racial micro/macroaggressions increased with no increase in support for Black teachers.

These Black teachers have been in the awkward positions of having to create lessons around police violence and being asked to share their thoughts and feelings about race with colleagues from different cultural and ethnic backgrounds. They did so while navigating a pandemic that shuttered schools and forced many into an unfamiliar way of teaching—online—and supporting youth also dealing with trauma, loss, and the fear and uncertainty triggered by social unrest. All this they did without mental health support systems, exacerbating already high levels of RBF.

While the current scholarship is insightful and applies name and substantiation to a condition that is innately felt by Black educators, more work is required in order to determine how RBF affects the socialization of Black K–12 teachers based on their school environments (Bristol, 2018) and how work-related racial stressors are compounded by explosive acts of system-sponsored anti-Blackness that are transmitted on a daily basis.

Interest Convergence

Derrick Bell coined the term "interest convergence" in his famous analysis of the motivation for the Supreme Court's *Brown v. Board of*

Education decision in 1954. Bell argued that social and political gains for People of Color are achieved only when those interests *converge* with the social and political interests of white people/supremacy (Ladson-Billings & Tate IV, 1995). So-called advances in racial justice can often be linked to motivations to advance white interests.

For example, though typically depicted as a symbol of America's shift toward morality and justice for Black people, *Brown v. Board of Education* was decided in favor of desegregation, Bell (1980) argued, because doing so would actually benefit the interests of (white) power. He pointed to the following factors as contributing to the *Brown* decision:

- The United States' strategic interests in the Cold War, particularly their need to win the loyalties of Black and Brown nations
- The need to minimize the risk of a domestic uprising in the aftermath of WWII, as Black veterans returned home with a (continuing) disinclination to accept second-class citizenship in the country they fought to protect
- The white elite's vested interest in desegregating the South, as Jim Crow segregation had become increasingly frowned upon worldwide, creating barriers to the country's economic success

Thus, Bell posited that despite the high regard many place on *Brown v. Board of Education* as an important landmark on the United States' continued quest toward racial justice, interest convergence explains the motivation for the actual decision itself.

Bell (1976) pushed the argument of interest convergence even further by highlighting the misalignment between "integration ideals" and the "educational interests" of Black students. Pointing to the inevitability of Black struggle to access high quality educational experiences in schools post-*Brown*, Bell found that the decision to integrate schools was one that actually harmed the Black community as Black teachers and administrators lost their jobs and Black children were bussed to schools to be educated by white teachers who held racist beliefs about Black students.

Yosso et al. (2021), in fact, conducted a quantitative study using data from the Early Childhood Longitudinal Study (ECLS) to look at how Black students perform in math when in predominantly Black spaces versus predominantly white spaces. They found that higher Black student test scores are related to a higher concentration of Black students at the school.

> Guided by CRT [critical race theory], in this study, we tested and con-
> firmed DuBois' 1935 hypothesis that Blacks need not attend integrated
> schools to succeed academically. We found that the increase in the Black
> student population was associated with the disappearance of the math-
> ematics performance gap between Black and White students. (p. 11)

Interestingly, they flip the tipping-point hypothesis on its ear. When
we refer to the tipping point in schools, we usually refer to the number
of Black students present that will cause white flight from the school
due to racist assumptions that Black students will bring down the rating of the school. Yosso et al. argue that we could instead use the
tipping-point mechanism to understand the number of Black students
present that will lead to increased academic excellence among Black
students. While integration is an important equity *vision*, the reality of
racism as a pandemic and anti-Black racism specifically means that to
serve Black students well we may need to decenter school integration
as a vehicle to Black academic, physical, and emotional well-being.

OUR OWN COUNTERSTORIES

Sade's Counterstory: Are Integrated Spaces Really Better for Black Students, Staff, and Faculty?

In considering Bell's argument, it is impossible for me to not question the likelihood that "separate but equal" would have been equal
at all. Had we known then what we know now, we may have been
better able to account for the traumatic impact of integration on Black
students and teachers, like the emergence of racial microaggressions
as a norm for Black students in the classroom. The impact of a white-
centered sociocultural context on Black students' motivation, performance, and identity in school has been well-documented, with Black
students systematically adultified, overdisciplined, labeled trouble-
some, expected less of academically, or plain ignored by their white
teachers (DeCuir-Gunby et al., 2012; Ferguson, 2000/2020; Kohli &
Solorzano, 2012; Walker et al., 2017). And the same school culture
that erodes the psyche and performance of Black students works just
as hard to weaken the resolve of Black educators. It seems like no
coincidence that the decision of *Brown v. Board of Education* led to the
removal of over 38,000 Black teachers from schools (Oakley et al.,
2009). The teaching force has yet to recover from this loss, which

means Black students rarely have the opportunity to be taught by Black teachers. Research has shown that Black students who had at least one Black teacher during or before elementary school are more likely to graduate high school, attend college, and perform better academically long term (Gershenson et al., 2017). It is unsurprising that with a scarcity of Black teachers and, at many schools, a scarcity of Black students, schools are often hostile places to be Black.

My own school experiences taught me that while a community of your peers can help with the micro-challenges of being Black in U.S. schools, it is not enough to solve them. The real challenge is entrenched within an education system and its norms—norms that prioritize white interests above the needs of the Black youth navigating the system, ultimately leaving us to fend for ourselves instead of setting us up to thrive.

As a former admissions counselor and Black affinity group leader at a predominantly white high school, I was uniquely positioned to observe interest convergence at play. My job was to sell the school in its best light and, to some degree, encourage Black students, in particular, to attend. The school, like most "elite" private schools, had a diversity problem: the majority of the students were white and from homogenous upper-class backgrounds. Part of my appeal as an admissions counselor was my visibility as a Black person, which I was expected to wield with the goal of attracting young Students of Color. It was a running joke among admissions staff in that network of schools that our teams usually contributed significantly to the campus diversity. I don't doubt that this trend is strategic.

By contrast, my other role as affinity group leader for the Black student association often made my work in admissions difficult. Black students shared with me the challenges of being Black at a predominantly white school. I eventually left the school, because the interest convergence was too evident: We often sought out Black students that the school had little intention to truly support. It doesn't look good for a school in the politically liberal Bay Area to be predominantly white. And yet, although diversity was prioritized and equity and inclusion were considered, belonging was a nonstarter; failure to belong was a marker of the Black experience on campus, for both Black students and Black staff.

I could write a full book about the microaggressions I witnessed and experienced at that school. There was the time when the students (who were not Black) devised a game meant to trick each other into saying the N-word, with no repercussions handed down from administration. Or the incident in which a Black student I worked with was casually called the N-word by someone they had considered a close friend, with that friend doubling down on their "right" to say it. I watched year after year as the school counseled out Students of Color who were deemed to be underperforming, while individual plans and tutoring sessions were arranged for underperforming white students. And once, in what became the final straw for me, I joined the handful of other Black staff at the front of the room at an all-school faculty meeting, where we'd been asked to tell the room all about our painful experiences of being a Black person in the school.

Watching the school repeatedly fumble calls to support Black students and staff, while also being too aware of its eagerness to recruit us for diversity clout, became more than my nerves could handle. I eventually encountered a crossroads that is familiar to many a Black educator: leave and save myself or sacrifice myself to try to be the support the students desperately needed. I ultimately chose the former, but not without much grief and post-traumatic stress.

Over the years, I've given much thought to what is gained and what is lost for Black people in predominantly white school settings. Is attending or working at such a school really what's best for us? As a Black student or teacher in predominantly white educational spaces, we have all considered Bell's defense of "separate but equal" in some form or another: Do the benefits of being in predominantly white spaces outweigh the costs? Are there any benefits to Black people, or are there only benefits to democratic values and integrationist visions? Racial harm lingers and insidiously permeates the way we think and feel about ourselves.

While we cannot undo integration, nor do I believe we should, we are overdue to reconcile the evidence that Black students and teachers are systematically harmed by the U.S. school system that upholds white hegemony. We must acknowledge the ugly truth that *Brown v. Board of Education* was not decided in the interest of Black people, so that we may reimagine our educational spaces. How do we transform these spaces to include the racial literacy needed to truly support Black students and teachers? This is a moral and ethical imperative, and an undertaking any educator that cares for Black students and Black peers must take on.

It is easy to undersell or overlook the impact of seemingly innocuous school rules and hierarchies. Black students often internalize their experiences, failing to see the way those experiences are patterned. Even Black educators can sometimes overlook their own complicity in

maintaining harmful status quos. Racial literacy can serve as a powerful tool of clarity for Black students and Black educators, to prevent
them from becoming consumed by the system designed to fail them.
As illustrated by the following story, the harm to Black educators and
students is multilayered, often taking years of reflection and self-
discovery before its depth is revealed even to ourselves.

Gertrude's Counterstory: Black Teacher Joy, One T-shirt at a Time

A few years ago, one of my students from Atlanta shared a story about
an experience he'd had back in middle school. It was the day after
the 2012 presidential election and the majority of Black students had
come to school with Barack Obama t-shirts. Presumably outraged by
this display of Black pride, the school administration ordered students
to turn their t-shirts inside-out, citing "political reasons" as a rationale.
My student recalls being saddened by the directive, but he acquiesced
along with the rest of the students. He remembers the embarrassment
of walking the halls with the seams of his shirt visible, something for
which his mother would have admonished him had he walked out of
his home in that fashion. However, at the end of the day, he ended
up having a memorable encounter with one of his Black teachers.
She quietly waved him toward the privacy of her classroom, opened
up her blazer, and revealed a hidden t-shirt bearing Barack Obama's
image over his campaign slogan of "change." They exchanged smiles
and a hug, then he left for home.

    Hearing my student's story, I could identify the directive of this
middle school administration as an attack on Black joy for both students and teachers. Politics aside, it should have come as no surprise
to the school administration that the re-electing of the first Black man
in the history of the nation to the presidency was a tremendous source
of pride for Black citizens all across the country. Surely, these school
leaders could have anticipated that students and teachers would want
to show that pride the subsequent Wednesday morning. Nonetheless,
school leaders were willing to coldly steal that joy, robbing from the
entire school an opportunity to embrace America's second wave of a
prospect for change, sending a loud message to anyone who wished
to engage in similar demonstrations. I was disheartened by the events
this student shared but had been working long enough in the school
system not to be surprised. However, for this student, this was ultimately a happy memory. The teacher who'd hidden her shirt under
the blazer was, in his mind, the hero of the narrative. I, though, as

a Black teacher, also see the ways that the teacher herself was also harmed by a policy that surveilled her and policed her clothing choices.

Anti-Blackness has an undeniable connection to school policy and reform. The inferior treatment of Black students and teachers in schools is a direct correlation to the still-ingrained notion that Black is equivalent to slave. As a result, anti-Blackness is systemized and allowed to thrive in institutional environments that boast neoliberal post-racialism (Dumas, 2016).

The position of Black teachers in schools is tenuous in situations such as these. How do you respond effectively when what is right and what is real are on opposite sides of the spectrum? In this particular case, this teacher was caught in a crossfire between her very real need to remain employed and her communal responsibility to Black students (and herself). The two, though, should never be at odds. And since Black educators do not operate monolithically, we find different ways to leverage our professional responsibilities with our moral sensibilities. This often results in various degrees of code-switching (Scott, 2003). For the teacher in this narrative, this manifested itself in an effort of subversive resistance.

On the surface, this act of camaraderie between student and teacher was an act of collective bravery in the face of institutional oppression. But it also contributed to the reproductive cycling that white fragility creates (Leonardo, 2004). The school said, in no uncertain terms:

Quiet your joy because white people are watching.
Quiet down because your brand of joy is unsavory and can be
   taken the wrong way.
Quiet that joy so the white adults won't get upset.
Quiet your joy so that your white classmates learn that you're
   nothing worth celebrating.
Quiet your joy so you don't get in trouble.
Quiet your joy so we all can remain safe.

We quiet ourselves to protect ourselves. It is the same act that our great-great-grandmothers used to protect their children in the slave quarters back on the plantation. Protecting ourselves means hiding our joy beneath blazers; sharing that joy means calling over Black students to witness that t-shirt beneath the blazer.

Back in 2016, when I taught in Atlanta, an issue arose regarding the handing out of Black Lives Matter (BLM) t-shirts among the student body. A student had been prevented from giving BLM shirts to other seniors with the alleged rationale that "BLM was a terrorist group." Within the hour, the details of this exchange had been shared across multiple student social media accounts, resulting in nearly 200 students staging a sit-in in the main foyer, blocking all access to classes during transition.

What ensued was a standoff between staff and students; some of the administrators and teachers pleaded with protesting students to get up and return to their classes. However, the students remained unmoved. It was the proudest moment I'd ever experienced as a teacher; I was brought to tears. Under the suspicious eyes of my coworkers, I made the decision to sit among the students in solidarity. An hour later, I was suspended, pending an investigation. After a long week filled with legal counsel and multiple written statements, I returned to my position; I returned, but even more jaded than I'd been before. The suspension didn't worry me—it wasn't my first rodeo fighting injustice at the district level. However, the factors that led up to it and everything that happened thereafter still keep me up at night.

What exactly do you do as a Black educator when situations like this arise on your school campus? How do you play your position if you're still left questioning which position you should play? My decision to sit with the students wasn't an easy one; my brain engaged in a mental tug-of-war. I knew every con of sitting; I'd weighed the option of being written up or fired. However, the cons had nothing on the energy of the youth in that hallway. In this small space, a microcosm of Black community arose, with all its variants. The protesting students held center stage; however, at the fringes, several factors of Black identity were at play. Behind me in the stairwell a group of young Black boys stood laughing and mocking some of the protesting students. Across from me, two Black boys decided to use the diversion as an opportunity to engage in a fight. And across from them, another boy gesturing toward the fight shouted desperately into the crowd, "Don't y'all see why this is pointless? Why should they care about respecting us? Look at what we do to each other!"

How does a Black educator perform the unassisted balancing act of carrying themselves and the weight of a moment like this? For me, sitting was the only option that would allow me to live with myself beyond that moment. The seated young people needed confirmation that they were right; the boys telling jokes in the back needed to be shown that this was no laughing matter; the fighting boys needed to see a teacher take a nonadversarial stance; and the boy who shouted into the crowd needed the message that we are indeed worthy, at all our intersections.

I currently teach at a small charter high school in California. My experience here is far different from my teaching experiences of the prior 11 years. For starters, this is the first school that has promoted a deep focus on cultivating faculty relationships. The faculty regularly participates in community circles, potlucks, and other school traditions. One such tradition is Faculty Fun; this is a 15-to-30-minute period where staff engage in various games. It didn't take long for me to realize how much I hated Faculty Fun. When you're painfully aware that you're the only Black person on the faculty, the "fun" hits a little differently.

One particular Faculty Fun will be etched in my memory forever. We were playing a game of Scattergories. A white twenty-something teacher was leading the game. I was critical of her in the way that I'm critical of all white people who work in urban schools, but I held nothing personally against her. In this very improvised game of Scattergories, she wrote a nondescript category on the board and, absent a letter die, picked a letter from her head. She cheered enthusiastically, "The Letter is 'N'"! Then with a cheeky smirk, she said, "Let's find all the 'N-Words.'" Just a week prior, I'd been called the N-word (with the hard "ER") by a white student. This game hit too close to home for me. I wanted to put a halt to the game immediately, to firmly implore her to choose another letter before she proceeded, but all I did was sit there frozen.

Racial microaggressions are a common occurrence in predominantly white-run school settings. It's a mystifying experience, felt the moment it's received. Yet your brain still goes about the work of second-guessing what your eyes, ears, and heart have already confirmed. Will you say something, or will you remain silent? My silence in that moment haunted me for several nights (and comes back to visit me on occasion).

Distance from this moment has reminded me that it was not solely on me to respond that day. Where were all the "good white folks" who had chosen to work at urban schools for the purpose of being instrumental during moments like these? Despite outwardly claiming a progressive stance, many white teachers engage in conversations and behaviors that avoid real discussions on race, swapping them for topics that are aligned with their comfort zones (Srivastava, 2005; Yoon, 2012). Whether they noticed it and chose silence or were oblivious to the moment entirely, each faculty member was culpable for the unchecked passing of that moment (Matias & Zemblyas, 2014).

A dear mentor once advised me not to go about the work of self-doubt when I find myself frozen on the receiving end of a microaggression; the freeze is the function and the form. Still, I sometimes revisit an alternate ending to that story, not to revel in what should have been, but rather to realize the many reasons I had for holding onto my silence in that moment. I was new to the school and even newer to the idea of being the only Black teacher in the building. When teachers who express the desire to be agents of change and equality are called out for maintaining hegemonic sensibilities, the hysterical presence of white fragility can be brutal (DiAngelo, 2018; Matias et al., 2016). That's an exhausting battle to fight on newly settled ground.

CONCLUSION

This chapter has identified only a fraction of the harm done to Black students and teachers when systemic anti-Blackness goes unchecked and is given life to breathe in our nation's schools. This chapter has been placed at the start of Part I to remind ourselves and our readers what is at stake when we leave unchecked the racism that runs rampant in schools. The purpose of this book is to share one possible approach to addressing a part of the problem—the lack of racial literacy of parenting and educating adults. Speaking to Black educators (and other Educators of Color), access to race theory can quite literally save lives. As bell hooks (1994) noted, having the language to describe what you experience and the historical and theoretical knowledge to make sense of it buoys you in the face of racial storms. Speaking to white educators and parenting adults, racial literacy can help counter the myths of white supremacy and tendencies to act on implicit bias (Eberhardt, 2019) while developing your own deeper understandings of historical, institutional, and structural racism.

REFERENCES

Acuff, J. (2018). Confronting racial battle fatigue and comforting my blackness as an educator. *Multicultural Perspectives, 20*(3), 174–181.

Barmore, P. (2021, May 24). *Black teachers ground down by racial battle fatigue after a year like no other. The Hechinger Report.*

Bell, D. (1976). Serving two masters: Integration ideals and client interests in school desegregation litigation. *The Yale Law Journal, 85*(4), 470–516.

Bell, D. (1980). *Brown v. Board of Education* and the interest-convergence dilemma. *Harvard Law Review, 93*(3), 518–533.

Bristol, T. J. (2018). To be alone or in a group: An exploration into how the school-based experiences differ for Black male teachers across one urban school district. *Urban Education, 53*(3), 334–354.

Chancellor, R. L. (2019). Racial battle fatigue: The unspoken burden of Black women faculty in LIS. *Journal of Education for Library and Information Science, 60*(3), 182–189.

DeCuir-Gunby, J. T., Martin, P. P., & Cooper, S. M. (2012). African American students in private, independent schools: Parents and school influences on racial identity development. *The Urban Review: Issues and Ideas in Public Education, 44*(1), 113–132.

DiAngelo, R. (2011). White fragility. *The International Journal of Critical Pedagogy, 3*(3), 54–70.

DiAngelo, R. (2018). *White fragility: Why it's so hard for white people to talk about racism.* Beacon Press.

Dumas, M. J. (2016). Against the dark: Antiblackness in education policy and discourse. *Theory into Practice, 55*(1), 11–19.

Eberhardt, J. (2019). *Biased: Uncovering the hidden prejudice that shapes what we see, think, and do.* Viking.

Ferguson, A. A. (2000/2020). *Bad boys: Public schools in the making of black masculinity.* University of Michigan Press.

Gershenson, S., Hart, C. M. D., Lindsay, C. A., & Papageorge, N. W. (2017). *The long-run impacts of same-race teachers* (IZA Discussion Paper Series No. 10630).

Hasan Hamilton, K. (n.d.). School-based racial battle fatigue. *Muslim Journal.* Retrieved June 20, 2022, from https://muslimjournal.net /racial-classroom-and-school-fatigue.

Hines III, M. T. (2016). The embeddedness of white fragility within white per-service principals' reflections on white privilege. *Critical Questions in Education, 7*(2), 130–145.

hooks, b. (1994). *Teaching to transgress: Education as the practice of freedom.* Routledge.

Ingersoll, R., Merrill, E., Stuckey, D., Collins, G., & Harrison, B. (2021). The demographic transformation of the teaching force in the United States. *Education Sciences, 11*(5), 234.

Jay, M. (2009). Race-ing through the school day: African American educators' experiences with race and racism in schools. *International Journal of Qualitative Studies in Education, 22*(6), 671–685.

Kohli, R. (2021). *Teachers of Color resisting racism and reclaiming education.* Harvard Education Press.

Kohli, R., & Solórzano, D. G. (2012). Teachers, please learn our names!: Racial microaggressions and the K-12 classroom. *Race Ethnicity and Education, 15*(4), 441–462.

Ladson-Billings, G., & Tate IV, W. F. (1995). Toward a critical race theory of education. *Teachers College Record, 97*(1), 47–68.

Leonardo, Z. (2004) The color of supremacy: Beyond the discourse of 'white privilege.' *Educational Philosophy and Theory, 36*(2), 137–152.

Matias, C. E., & DiAngelo, R. (2013). Beyond the face of race: Emo-cognitive explorations of white neurosis and racial cray-cray. *Educational Foundations, 27*(3–4), 3–20.

Matias, C. E., Montoya, R., & Nishi, N. W. (2016). Blocking CRT: How the emotionality of whiteness blocks CRT in urban teacher education. *Educational Studies, 52*(1), 1–19.

Matias, C. E., & Zembylas, M. (2014). "When saying you care is not really caring": Whiteness and the role of disgust. *Journal of Critical Studies in Education, 55*(3), 319–337.

Oakley, D., Stowell, J., & Logan, J. R. (2009). The impact of desegregation on Black teachers in the metropolis, 1970–2000. *Ethnic and Racial Studies, 32*(9), 1576–1598.

Okello, W. K., Quaye, S. J., Allen, C., Carter, K. D., & Karikari, S. N. (2020). "We wear the mask": Self-definition as an approach to healing from racial battle fatigue. *Journal of College Student Development, 61*(4), 422–438.

Pizarro, M., & Kohli, R. (2018). "I stopped sleeping": Teachers of Color and the impact of racial battle fatigue. *Urban Education, 55*(7), 967–991.

Scott, K. A. (2003). My students think I'm Indian: The presentation of an African-American self to pre-service teachers. *Race, Ethnicity and Education, 6*(3), 211–226.

Smith, W. A. (2004). Black faculty coping with racial battle fatigue: The campus racial climate in a post-civil rights era. In D. Cleveland (Ed.), *A long way to go: Conversations about race by African American faculty and graduate students* (pp. 171–190). Peter Lang.

Smith, W. A. (2008). Higher education: Racial battle fatigue. In R. T. Schaefer (Ed.), *Encyclopedia of race, ethnicity, and society* (pp. 615–618). Sage Publications.

Smith, W. A., Hung, M., & Franklin, J. D. (2011). Racial battle fatigue and the MisEducation of Black men: Racial microaggressions, societal problems, and environmental stress. *Journal of Negro Education, 80*(1), 63–82.

Smith, W. A., Yosso, T. J., & Solórzano, D. G. (2006). Challenging racial battle fatigue on historically white campuses: A critical race examination of race-related stress. In C. A. Stanley (Ed.), *Faculty of Color: Teaching in predominantly white colleges and universities* (pp. 299–327). Anker Publishing.

Srivastava, S. (2005). "You're calling me a racist?" The moral and emotional regulation of antiracism and feminism. *Signs: Journal of Women in Culture and Society, 31*(1), 29–62.

Trent, M., Dooley, D. G., & Dougé, J. (2019). The impact of racism on child and adolescent health. *Pediatrics, 144*(2), 1–14.

Viesca, K. M., Matias, C. E., Garrison-Wade, D., Tandon, M., & Galindo, R. (2014). "Push it real good." The challenge of disrupting dominant discourses regarding race in teacher education. *Critical Education, 5*(11).

Walker, D., Matias, C. E., & Brandehoff, R. (2017). *"Who you callin' smart-mouth?" Misunderstood traumatization of Black and Brown girls* (Occasional Paper Series 38, Vol. 2017, Article 6). Bank Street.

Yoon, I. H. (2012). The paradoxical nature of whiteness-at-work in the daily life of schools and teacher communities. *Race Ethnicity and Education, 15*(5), 587–613.

Yosso, T. J., Smith, W. A., Solórzano, D. G., & Hung, M. (2021). A critical race theory test of W.E.B. DuBois' hypothesis: Do Black students need separate schools? *Race Ethnicity and Education, 25*(3), 370–388.

CHAPTER 2

Building on the Antiracism Work of Others

Racial Literacy Educators and Organizations

Kimberly Williams Brown

The work of RISE for Racial Justice occurs in concert with the significant labor, pedagogical brilliance, and fierce talent and commitment of other racial literacy educators and organizations. This chapter acknowledges, celebrates, and raises the visibility of a few prominent racial literacy educators and organizations who do this work. Along with my coauthors of this book, I recognize that there are others laboring in this vein whom we do not have the space to share or about whose work we have yet to hear; this does not diminish, of course, the importance of their work, and we hope that future work will more thoroughly acknowledge organizations in this field.

I offer this chapter as a living organizational "review" in lieu of a traditional literature review. There are very few reviews of racial literacy organizations, and, of those that exist, these reviews take the form of evaluations of specific public racial literacy organizations (see Brown & Mazza, 1996, for example). Other reviews of these organizations are in the form of reports. For example, Shapiro (2002), with the support of the Aspen Institute, produced a report that described 10 public racial literacy programs. The purpose of the report was to guide companies in selecting a training program for their employees by providing an in-depth description and comparison across 10 well-known programs.

Using purposeful sampling, I focused on five organizations that have at least 10 years of experience providing racial literacy workshops to the public (in person and/or remotely) and that launched a purposeful public racial literacy campaign during 2020. The organizations selected are the National Coalition Building Institute (NCBI), The People's Institute for Survival, Intergroup Dialogue, the Othering and Belonging Institute, and Race Forward.

Atypically, this chapter also reviews self-guided curricula offered by five books: *The Inner Work of Racial Justice* (Magee, 2019), *Me and White Supremacy* (Saad, 2020), *So You Want to Talk About Race* (Oluo, 2018), *How to Be an Antiracist* (Kendi, 2019), and *Mindful of Race* (King, 2018). These books include a number of exercises, engaging the reader in learning about racism and reflecting on prior racialized experiences. I include these books because, I believe, they also act as antiracism training (particularly for this moment of pandemic isolation).

All organizations and books were studied to learn more about their work and their approach to racial literacy training. In addition, their advertising materials, organizational structure, and course offerings were analyzed. This chapter shares the results of this review as well as characteristics common to this form of public scholarship and public pedagogy.

PUBLIC RACIAL LITERACY ORGANIZATIONS

The organizations that I highlight in this chapter, as forbearers and contemporaries in this work, recognize that teaching about race requires a specific way to engage in the process of racial literacy through practices of community engagement. Racial literacy could easily be mistaken as the ability to read and write about race. While this of course is a part of racial literacy, it is not the full story. To be literate in race—and, in particular, to read and write about race—is devoid of the affective and communal experiences necessary for healing and growth. These public racial literacy organizations remind us that because racism is institutional and structural, it takes a collective effort to dismantle it. Therefore, the "public" in public racial literacy has always been positioned as a practice in, of, and by the community.

National Coalition Building Institute

I begin with one of the oldest racial literacy organizations, the National Coalition Building Institute. NCBI began with the desire of its founder, Cherie Brown, to create "effective models for combatting racism and other forms of discrimination by combining methods of individual emotional healing with strategies for community activism" (Brown &

Mazza, 1996, p. 391). Brown recognized that individual healing—the ability to identify and work through trauma that impeded one's ability to be in community—is necessary for a person to participate in antidiscriminatory work. Brown also recognized that antiracist work is only possible in a community of practice dedicated to activist work. Brown's lifework put in conversation Black and Jewish people who worked across their differences in strategic ways to develop racial literacy. To do this, Brown modeled working across differences of age, gender, religion, class, and other social markers in her relationship with Lou Smith, a Black man with whom she first collaborated as a teenager and with whom she later worked.

One key feature of a public racial literacy organization is that its growth is determined by the demand of the public. The demand for NCBI workshops grew exponentially from its beginning in 1984 so that within a few short years, there were chapters of NCBI across the United States. Brown did not intend to grow a national organization when she began having these conversations as a teenager, but that growth was inevitable after the public took interest in what was possible through the conversations and workshops offered by NCBI. Due to the insidiousness of race and racism in the United States, there are particular moments when public racial literacy organizations grow exponentially. The 1990s were such a time for NCBI (as was 2020 for the RISE for Racial Justice organization and other racial literacy organizations).

I write here at length about NCBI not because it is the first or the only organization to engage in racial literacy work but because NCBI's strategic growth as a leader in racial literacy and as a racial literacy organization must be named and marked as important foregrounding for the growth of other groups. Revolutionary thinking and practices have long existed alongside racism and discriminatory practices. In fact, there have been many intellectual thought leaders from whom Brown and others have pulled, such as the Combahee River Collective, Patricia Hill Collins, bell hooks, W. E. B. Dubois, James Baldwin, and C. L. R. James. But while they provided the theoretical and activist frameworks for racial literacy, the community, ground-up, working-across-difference approach practiced by NCBI foregrounds the work that the authors of this book have designed in founding RISE for Racial Justice.

The People's Institute for Survival and Beyond: Undoing Racism

The People's Institute (Shapiro, 2002) was founded by Rob Chisom and Jim Dunn in 1980 to build an antiracist, multicultural movement for social change. The People's Institute is invested in addressing systemic racism by defining terms, using a common language, and engaging an analytical framework for dismantling racist systems. Like NCBI, the People's Institute is grounded in principles of communal engagement through activist work from the 1960s and 1970s. The organization has four regional offices in Louisiana, California, New York, and Washington State. It primarily engages in its work through a two-day workshop called "Undoing Racism," which examines the sociological, historical, and community activist approaches to the study of race and racism.

The Undoing Racism workshop model focuses on disempowerment and systemic racism rather than the emotional responses that people have to engaging in antiracist work. The model challenges participants to be responsible, active, and accountable for creating antiracist spaces. The model asks that individuals struggle with organizing in their own communities. In particular, the model explores "language and definitions for understanding racism and examines how traditional views of intergroup relations such as 'melting pot' theories and 'colorblind' policies have ignored and denied racism in the United States. Final discussions focus on community and institutional transformation and the leadership role of participants after the training" (Shapiro, 2002, p. 12).

As a public racial literacy organization, the People's Institute implores leaders who participate in the two-day workshops to be responsible for their actions by not being gatekeepers to white supremacy. The other strengths of this public racial literacy organization are being accountable to the communities in which it works and *for* whom it works. Although the trainings serve white people, the workshops are also useful for BIPOC as they provide "both content and methods that are reflective of and appealing to many communities of color" (Shapiro, 2002, p. 12).

Intergroup Dialogue

Intergroup dialogue (IGD) is a critical dialogical strategy that promotes engagement across cultural and social divides, fostering learning about social diversity and inequalities and cultivating an ethos of social responsibility (Zúñiga, 2003). IDG is a 35-year-old, research-based program that was initially designed for college campuses, but is now widely used in P–12 settings as well as in corporate and organizing spaces.

Although IGD is a framework and not an organization, I use it here as a racial literacy organization because it was developed in the 1980s at the University of Michigan, Ann Arbor, in a moment when there was much social unrest on college and university campuses. I find this model useful because of its origins in activist critical scholarship in the disciplines of psychology, sociology, education, communication, social work, and Women's and Gender Studies. It is specifically grounded in the critical pedagogy of Freire (1970), the critical multicultural education model (Banks, 1993), and critical race theory (Delgado & Stefancic, 2012). IGD, although not applied the same in all settings, has eight distinct features:

1. Listening
2. Learning
3. Face-to-face interaction (although this has been modified in 2020 to accommodate the COVID-19 pandemic and remote instruction requirements)
4. Sustained dialogue
5. Facilitation by trained people
6. Surfacing conflict
7. Deepening understanding of shared reality
8. Recognizing human dignity

Although IGD is primarily used on college campuses as part of co-curricular programming or as part of the curricular offerings, it is also used in P–12 settings with high school "near-peer" students and adult facilitators (Kaplowitz et al., 2019). To a lesser extent and anecdotally, the IGD model is used in community organizations to build community and to use the skills of listening, facilitating, and organizing. On college campuses, the structures of the various models are different across campuses (see the Introduction for its use at Vassar College), but they typically include someone who directs/leads the program and someone who manages the logistics of creating dialogue spaces, selecting participants, and managing the group size and demographics. The size and demographics of a group are important because they allow equity of participation and space for participants to not be "the only" representative of a particular group.

IGD spaces are co-facilitated (not taught), with special attention to the dominant and subjugated identities of the facilitators. There is an emphasis on developing "good" facilitation skills such as having content and process knowledge, being self-aware and committed to learning, being prepared but flexible, not avoiding conflict, appropriately sharing stories, and equalizing power dynamics in dialogue. For IGD facilitation, it is not enough to know the material, but it is important to know it and yourself well enough to be flexible and thoughtful.

Multiple ways of knowing are also embraced and encouraged so that the intellectual tradition of knowing cerebrally is not privileged. Some of the other ways of knowing through embodiment and emotion are important in dialogue spaces. A wide range of emotions are embraced in the IGD space because emotions are experienced as another way of knowing (though emotions are not used to manipulate or to silence others).

The Othering and Belonging Institute

The Othering and Belonging Institute is housed at the University of California, Berkeley, through a grant named for Walter and Evelyn Haas, Jr. The institute, formerly known as the Haas Institute for a Fair and Inclusive Society, brings together diverse people across multiple communities to ask questions about exclusion and belonging with the goal of creating a just society that provides caring communities for people. For the institute, "belonging describes values and practices where no person is left out of our circle of concern. Belonging means more than just having access; it means having a meaningful voice and the opportunity to participate in the design of political, social, and cultural structures. Belonging includes the right to both contribute and make demands upon society and political institutions" (2022).

Established in 2012, the institute works with and through issues that require short-term action and long-term planning. The institute engages in communication strategy and arts that reframe the dominant narrative geared at control and fear to narratives that celebrate the human spirit and human connectedness.

john a. powell is the founder and director of the Othering and Belonging Institute. The institute engages faculty, students, and community members through seven clusters of concentrated work and research: disability studies, diversity and health disparities, economic disparities, LGBTQ citizenship, race, diversity and educational policy, and religious diversity. These clusters house faculty from a variety of the schools and colleges at UC Berkeley who align their research with community activists and policymakers. In a 2019 report, the institute found five ways in which they made a significant impact:

1. Offering responsive research
2. Shifting public discourse
3. Contributing to policy and practice
4. Focusing on campus climate
5. Building an ecosystem of belonging

The institute hosts a conference every 2 years to bring together scholars, artists, activists, and community members to encourage deep connections and relationship building (though, they moved to a remote annual offering during COVID-19). The institute, in its 10 years of operation, has greatly impacted policy, community, research, and activism.

Race Forward

Race Forward was founded in 1981 and brings a systematic analysis and an innovative approach to complex issues around race and racism. They have a large executive staff of approximately 55 members who organize and run the day-to-day operations of the organization. They united with the Center for Social Inclusion in 2017. Together, the organization, originally called the Applied Research Center, catalyzes movement building for racial justice. The organization houses the Government Alliance on Race and Ethnicity (GARE), which is an alliance of local governments working to achieve racial equity. They host a daily news site called *Colorlines*, and a conference called *Facing Race*, the country's largest multicultural conference on race.

The work of Race Forward is organized in three ways: through research, media, and practice. Race Forward conducts research on race by providing deeper levels of understanding about systems of oppression. Although their research highlights interpersonal racial disparity, they focus primarily on systematic racism while trying to understand how race compounds and impacts other societal issues. Race Forward also uses media through *Colorlines* to bring a critical race lens to reporting the news. Finally, Race Forward organizes its work through practice by mobilizing, skill building, leadership development, organization and alliance building, issue framing, messaging, and advancing solutions. Training and consulting services are provided in the areas listed above through the Race Forward Leadership Action Network online and in person, and they are well-known for their racial literacy workshops—Building Racial Equity (which looks beyond interpersonal forms of racism to focus on institutional and structural racism), Organizing Racial Equity, and Decision Making for Racial Equity. They also have speakers who provide talks to large national audiences. The Race Forward conference is held biennially and attracts activists, speakers, artists, and student, among others. Their most recent public literacy campaign was "drop the I word" to promote dropping the term "illegal" in reference to immigrants.

Equity Literacy Institute

The Equity Literacy Institute divides its work into five areas: (1) customized professional learning and workshops, (2) customized online professional development training, (3) equity coaching and leadership support, (4) equity visioning and strategic planning, and (5) equity facilitator training. The Equity Literacy framework builds capacity for knowledge and skills that enables their work to be a threat to inequality. Their goal through equity literacy, rather than diversity or cultural training, is to help people identify subtle forms of discrimination.

The customized professional workshops use seven distinct designs to engage participants. Although they customize workshops based on participant need, the following designs capture broadly the workshops most often offered:

1. Introductory and framework building
2. Curricular
3. Pedagogical or instructional
4. Institutional transformation
5. Issue-specific
6. Equity leadership development
7. Facilitator training and "train-the-trainer" sessions

These sessions engage participants new to the topic of race with introductory information about antiracism; more advanced coursework engages those who want to hone their skills as trainers and facilitators themselves.

The customized online professional development training has the capacity for web training, which can be short-term trainings or scaffolded over 2 years. There are also self-paced modules that allow participants to learn independently. The self-paced curriculum is designed to introduce people to basic concepts like equity and bias, and also includes issue-specific modules on social identities like race, gender class, disability, and so on, as well as role-specific modules for teachers, leaders, student services personnel, district-level administrators, and others.

There are three ways in which one may engage with the program—through equity coaching, equity visioning and strategic planning, and equity facilitator training. These advanced sessions are designed to build on already acquired competences. Equity coaches meet one-on-one or in small groups with participants to strengthen equity competences and abilities. The equity visioning and strategic planning area works with institutions to do long-term visioning around equity statements and institutional change. The train-the-trainer area uses advanced content along with knowledge about putting workshops together and skills and strategies for working with difficult participants.

SELF-GUIDED CURRICULA: THE BOOKS

In this review, I focus on several books that were published in 2018–2020: *The Inner Work of Racial Justice* (Magee, 2019), *Me and White Supremacy* (Saad, 2020), *So You Want to Talk About Race* (Oluo, 2018), *How to Be an Antiracist* (Kendi, 2019), and *Mindful of Race* (King, 2018). I selected these five texts because all took on increasing relevance and readership during 2020 (two recognized as *New York Times* bestsellers), are nonfiction, include autobiographical pieces, and are pedagogical in purpose and writing. I identify these as public racial literacy texts because of the work they do to define, create space for, and complicate conversations about race, racism, racial trauma, and healing.

The Inner Work of Racial Justice

Rhonda Magee's important work sits at the intersection of racial justice and mindfulness by making the argument that racial justice is not effective without also being mindful of the ways in which we carry in our bodies the tensions and traumas of racial harm. In other words, she says racial justice is one way of living mindfully. The book advocates for mindful racial justice because it "seeks to alleviate not merely isolated incidents of racial suffering, but all suffering caused by racism—including suffering that is hard to see" (Magee, 2019, p. 20). Magee makes clear that mindful racial justice literacy is as much about seeing, understanding, and believing what is quantifiable as it is about what is not easily seen, spoken, understandable, or quantifiable.

Magee's book models the beautiful ways in which racial literacy is a complex analytic by using autobiographical self-disclosures about her experiences with race, as well as narrating stories of former students and their experiences and confusions about race and racism. She uses these stories as entry points for us to think about our own questions around race and to provide us with literacy tools after she shares the stories and their impact. These stories, coupled with definitions and mindfulness exercises, make the text accessible to a wide readership.

Me and White Supremacy

Layla Saad's book is a guide to white people engaging and re-engaging in self-work around race. The book was originally a challenge by Saad on Instagram to white people to document their racist thoughts and behaviors. The Instagram campaign #MeandWhiteSupremacy asked white people to document in a workbook these thoughts and behaviors through a step-by-step reflection process. The aim of the workbook was to help white people to understand their white privilege and to stop their participation in white supremacy. Saad asks readers and participants to examine themselves and their proximity to white supremacy closely.

The workbook, now a published book, is divided into parts. Part I, called "Welcome to the Work," is divided into six chapters. Part II, called "The Work," is divided into four weeks and a "What Now" section. The appendix is a call to being in community after 28 days of individual self-work. The appendix also details how to set up circles to be in conversation and community. The resources section boasts a robust glossary that defines terms described in the book. Finally, there is a section for further reading.

Saad's book is a text that emerged from a public racial campaign. The text itself is a public racial literacy text that guides white people on a self-journey to understanding their own whiteness and white supremacy. However, like the other self-guided books in this section, there is personal autobiographical narrative that punctuates the text and demonstrates the importance of doing personal antiracist work and the power of the journey to those stories.

So You Want to Talk About Race

Ijeoma Oluo writes about the everyday questions and conversations people have about race. She uses her personal experiences and the relationships with people in her life to engage with complex (and often confusing) ideas about race. The book is divided into seventeen chapters with each chapter posed as a question about race. For example, Chapter 2 asks, "What is racism?"; Chapter 6 asks, "Is police brutality really about race?"; and Chapter 9 asks, "Why can't I say the 'N' word?" The book also provides a discussion guide for its readers.

Like the other texts I have explored, Oluo's book captures the complexities of racism that are interpersonal, structural, political, and social. The text is accessible and written for those who enter this conversation for the first time to grasp and grapple with concepts they may have heard but not fully understood. In that way, the text is a public racial literacy text because Oluo, a public intellectual and racial literacy educator, put into popular circulation definitions of words and concepts that sometimes only live in the enclaves of the academy.

One of the most riveting stories told in the book is the story of the first time Oluo is called the N-word. She describes a moment when she was 11 when she and her brother spent time with her mother's friend for a week. She describes having a good time on the weekend with her mother's friends' children, but it is the incident that happened on the school bus the following week that stayed with her for a long time. She painfully describes how the classmates of the friends with whom she stayed called them the "N" word and laughed at them. It is a moment that stays with the reader because it sits in this uncomfortable space that children inhabit—a space where they know racism is bad and it feels awful when it happens to them, but they do not always know what to do about it or what to call it. They do not always share with the adults in their lives the trauma of racism being leveraged at them by people they sometimes know and trust. This story gets at the deeply personal and lifelong struggle of BIPOC with racism and the trauma they process at young ages and that is nearly invisible to the white teachers, friends, and colleagues around them.

As a public racial literacy text, this book speaks candidly to all of us about what it feels like to be assaulted with racism at a variety of levels. Oluo brings home how it is we each can be more thoughtful and careful about how we develop our antiracist practices.

How to Be an Antiracist

Ibram X. Kendi's book is a how-to guide about what is and is not racism and how to become an antiracist person. The book uses personal narrative, definitions, and a new way of thinking about and talking through racism.

What Kendi offers is a new and energizing way to think about working toward antiracism instead of working against racism. Instead of accusing people of being racist, he suggests we ask if they are antiracist. Kendi makes the argument in the text that people get upset when called "racist" and it jars them into defensiveness. If we want people to be open about talking about how they are implicated in racism, Kendi says we have to be clear about our definitions and that those who are offended by the word "racist" should examine why and think about whether their actions and practices are in fact antiracist.

The definitions of racist and antiracist Kendi uses—"One who is supporting a racist policy through their actions or inactions or expressing a racist idea" and "One who is supporting an antiracist policy through their actions or expressing an antiracist idea"—are easily understood and are not accusatory. They invite people to pose questions for themselves about whether they are working for or against racist policies. The significance of these definitions is that they vary from popular definitions such as the definition of racism as power plus prejudice (which is the definition we prefer in our training). It also invites readers to think about their actions critically without the weight of the word "racist."

As a public racial literacy text, its effectiveness lies in its accessibility and the slight variation with which we are invited to think about racism and, more importantly, antiracism. The book is divided into 18 chapters that cover topics such as power, color, and survival. Kendi's book is a *New York Times* bestseller and became increasingly popular in 2020 as the United States and the world grappled with anti-Black racism; a racist, white nationalist president and his followers; and COVID-19, which killed more BIPOC in the United States than any other disease.

Mindful of Race

Ruth King's text posits that racism is a "dis-ease," but one that is curable. Through accessible language and pulling from current events, King makes connections across different time periods in the United States to make the argument that white supremacy is circuitous and often shows up in similar ways across contexts. For example, she tells the story of Dylann Roof, the Confederate loyalist who on June 17, 2015, killed nine Black church worshippers in the Emanuel African

Methodist Episcopal Church in Charleston, South Carolina. King connects this incident to one that took place on June 16, 1822, when Denmark Vesey, a preacher, was suspected of planning a slave rebellion. When white citizens suspected that this rebellion against slavery was happening, they hanged 35 Black people and burned the church down. These two incidents occurred 193 years apart almost to the day.

What is most powerful about this book is that King shares with us not only her expertise in clinical psychology, organizational development, and diversity consulting but also her expertise in mindfulness-based meditation, which she says is a social psychology that supports experiences of well-being and the best way to transform our relationship to racial suffering. By documenting her own experience of open-heart surgery at age 20 because of her rage about racism, she extends the medical metaphor throughout the book to help us imagine how we might rid ourselves of the disease of racism.

The book is divided into three parts. The three parts of the book follow the heart surgery metaphor so that the book goes on the medical journey the author experienced but with racism as the disease. She also addresses the emotional and spiritual impact of racism in addition to its physical effect. Explicitly described as a mindful practice is saying the names of the Black men and boys who died senselessly at the hands of the police—inhaling as the name is being read, and after each of their names exhaling. That practice and others make this text unusual and clear about its purpose to use mindfulness-based practices as a cure to the racist traumas we experience.

CONCLUSION

The public racial literacy organizations and books I explored in this chapter differ in tone, structure, and the details of what they offer. They are similar in their attempt to give us language, to name experiences explicitly, to create space, and to think about healing the traumas of racial injustice and violence. I highlight them in this book because they have enriched our work with RISE for Racial Justice. It is not to say we agree with all the ways the authors have presented their ideas or all the ways in which the work happens in these organizations. But it is to say that we appreciate that these organizations and authors have walked this difficult antiracist path. We honor them for being in struggle at a personal cost we understand too intimately—the cost of our health, sometimes our sanity, and our time. We appreciate their generosity in making transparent their processes so we may learn from them, build on their work, and offer a version of this work that pulls people in to see themselves and to make personal as well as systemic change.

REFERENCES

Banks, J. A. (1993). The canon debate, knowledge construction, and multicultural education. *Educational Researcher, 22*(5), 4–14.

Brown, C. R., & Mazza, G. J. (1996). Anti-racism, healing and community activism. *The Humanistic Psychologist, 24*(3), 391–402.

Delgado, R., & Stefancic, J. (2012). *Critical race theory: An introduction* (2nd ed.). NYU Press.

Freire, P. (1970). *Pedagogy of the oppressed.* Continuum Publishing.

Kaplowitz, D. R., Griffin, S. R., & Seyka, S. (2019). *Race dialogues: A facilitator's guide to tackling the elephant in the classroom.* Teachers College Press.

Kendi, I. X. (2019). *How to be an antiracist.* Random House.

King, R. (2018). *Mindful of race: Transforming racism from the inside out.* Sounds True.

Magee, R. (2019). *The inner work of racial justice: Healing ourselves and transforming our communities through mindfulness.* TarcherPerigee.

Othering and Belonging Institute at U.C. Berkeley. (2019). *Expanding the circle of human concern: Impact report.* Accessed June 27, 2022, from https://belonging.berkeley.edu/sites/default/files/expanding_the_circle_of_human_concern_impact_report.pdf.

Othering and Belonging Institute at U.C. Berkeley. (2022). *Bridging and belonging.* Accessed June 27, 2022, from https://belonging.berkeley.edu/bridging-belonging.

Oluo, I. (2018). *So you want to talk about race.* Basic Books.

Saad, L. (2020). *Me and white supremacy: Combat racism, change the world, and become a good ancestor.* Sourcebooks.

Shapiro, I. (2002). *Training for racial equity and inclusion: A guide to selected programs.* The Aspen Institute. Accessed on June 21, 2022, from https://www.aspeninstitute.org/wp-content/uploads/files/content/docs/pubs/training_racial_equity.pdf.

Zúñiga, X. (2003). Bridging differences through dialogue about campus. *About Campus: Enriching the Student Learning Experience, 7*(6), 8–16.

Part II

NARRATIVES FROM THE FIELD

In this part, Chapters 3–8 use narrative autoethnography to provide an overview of the courses offered through RISE for Racial Justice. Each narrative describes the facilitator's journey into antiracism training, provides an overview of the course design, and addresses critical moments of challenge and promise faced across conceptualizing, designing, implementing, and facilitating. Each chapter ends with lessons learned and recommendations for future iterations of the course. These narratives extend our understandings about pedagogical applications of racial literacy courses for educators, parenting adults, and student populations in schools.

Chapter 3 focuses on the development, design, and teaching of RISE for Racial Justice's signature introductory course, How to Talk About Race (HTAR). This course is offered for educators and parents and was taught remotely during the 2020–2021 COVID-19 pandemic. Chapters 4–6 share the three intermediate courses offered by RISE for Racial Justice—Race Theory, Community of Reflective Practice, and Intergroup Dialogue Pedagogy. Chapters 7 and 8 explore two antiracism courses in affinity spaces—one for young people (high school students) and the other for white womxn.

CHAPTER 3

Introducing Race and Racism to Educators and Parenting Adults

An Overview of Our Signature Course

Colette N. Cann

This chapter offers an overview of the history, development, and design of RISE for Racial Justice's signature introductory course, How to Talk About Race (lovingly referred to as HTAR). This course is offered for parenting adults and educators in K–12 schools across the United States (though we have occasionally also had grandparents, aunties/uncles, and faculty in higher education join as well). Initially, as explained in the Introduction, HTAR was designed and offered to K–12 teachers in a small upstate town in New York in response to rising tensions between white educators and BIPOC youth after the 2016 presidential election outcome in the United States. At its inception, the course served roughly 20 teachers each semester and was offered in person at a local college after school on Fridays. The course, books, and materials were free, and participants ate dinner together during class. The course was held for 6 weeks (3 hours per meeting) and taught by myself and another experienced facilitator, Robin Alpern.

Five years later, following global racial protests against state violence targeted at Black people and despite a new president in the White House, the United States continues to struggle with white supremacy, bold and blatant in both its insurrection at the Capital and attack on critical race theory (CRT). We offered this course 10 times during the 2020–2021 academic year, and all sections of the course were taught remotely by interracial teams of 2 or 3 (brilliant and fierce) facilitators. While the structure of the course has remained unchanged since the course's inception, the examples used to illustrate concepts shift constantly in response to the everchanging landscape of racism in and out of schools.

This chapter provides an in-depth description of the structure of this "founding" course. Critical to this course is the teaching of tools (or techniques) for how to *read* and make sense of this racialized world, how to *talk* to others about race, and how to *write* our own visions of racial justice collectively in community. Over the course of six class sessions, we introduce several such tools such as the use of norms specific to building a community that can sustain difficult dialogues about race, the use of mindful listening, a self-diagnostic to introduce mindfulness and self-awareness into racial justice work, and race theory to recognize that ongoing knowledge building is a critical part of racial literacy. Using a common pedagogical framework—the four levels of racism—we explore as a community the use of these tools as we build our capacity for sustained dialogues about race and racism. This chapter also provides a peek at several antiracism practices that educators (and parenting adults) can use with youth to address internalized, cultural, interpersonal, and institutional racism.

THE BIRTH OF HTAR: A BRIEF HISTORY

In fall 2016, the 45th president was elected. I recall going to bed that evening huddled under the covers with my daughter, both of us scared about the outcome; he was predicted to win by 8:00 P.M. on election night. When I woke up the next day, I grabbed my phone off the nightstand and googled "presidential election." He'd won. My daughter awoke to me crying. "What's wrong, mom?" she asked. To this day, I'm not sure how I should have answered that. I simply said, "We lost the election, baby." By "we" I didn't mean our political party had lost. I meant Black people, I meant womxn, I meant the queer and trans community, I meant those without their basic needs met, I meant our environment. But I also meant white people, cis straight men, middle-class people. All of us lost in that election, even those who thought they'd won. Of course, at that time, we did not know a pandemic of the magnitude of COVID-19 was coming, but we knew the pandemics of racism, sexism, capitalist greed and excess, and environmental degradation (to name a few) would intensify and variants, old and new, would arise. We just didn't know the genetic code of each variant yet.

At a local public school, a white teacher in a predominantly Black and Brown school district decided to open her class meeting the day after the election with words of celebration and warning to her BIPOC students, "Now you're going to get what you have coming to you. Finally, someone is going to hold you accountable to high standards. You won't be able to get away with things anymore." We can only wonder what she thought they'd been getting away with when a Black man was the president. And we can only imagine what she thought they had coming to them. But her words came to the college education department where I taught through one of our student teachers who had been standing in the back of the classroom appalled at what she heard.

In spring 2017, I decided to design a beginning course in race, racism, and schools for K–12 educators. In that moment, I wanted to offer an opportunity for teachers to increase their racial literacy so that they could better make sense of the political and racial moment. We offered such a course at my higher education institution, but it was held before 3:00 P.M. and teachers could not attend (it was also prohibitively expensive, and the college refused to allow local K–12 teachers to enroll in courses for credit without paying the exorbitant tuition). I reached out to the author of Chapter 8 in this book, Robin Alpern, a white antiracism trainer who was teaching at an antiracism training organization, the Center for the Study of White American Culture (CSWAC), to partner with me to teach the course.

I designed a 6-week course that met for 3 hours on consecutive Fridays. Funding was procured from a committee at my institution that supported projects bringing the campus and surrounding community into relationship. This funding was used to purchase books, materials, and dinner for participating teachers; the course was offered from 4:00–7:00 P.M. and many teachers came directly from school without having eaten.

The course uses a four-levels-of-racism pedagogical framework (Cann & DeMeulenaere, 2020) and is rooted in one of the tenets of critical race theory—racism is everyday and endemic to the United States. That is, racism is not always an extraordinary act of physical violence (though it also is); it can be more subtle and difficult to see. It is ever operating. By teaching the multiple levels of racism, we teach about its multiple manifestations—providing a lens for teachers to see what has always been there.

For many teachers, racism is defined as one person saying to another person something "objectively" racist—the use of the N-word or that you don't like children with a specific racial identity. In other words, some teachers believe that racism is only intentional acts meant to hurt someone's feelings. It is ugly, impolite, and not something they would ever do. The purpose of HTAR is to show the many ways racism shows up in classrooms and schools intentionally and unintentionally, interpersonally, and institutionally, and how it harms BIPOC families (and white families, though differently of course). As I explain in the next section, teaching about the four levels of racism is one way to show other manifestations of racism in classrooms and schools.

THE PEDAGOGICAL FRAMEWORK

Like many antiracism organizations (such as Race Forward), educators (such as Kevin Kumashiro), and resources (such as Adams & Bell, 2016; Tatum, 1997/2017), we use the four levels of racism (here, "levels" means "types") as a pedagogical framework for HTAR. Elsewhere, I have defined a pedagogical framework as an organizing schema that holds concepts together (Cann & DeMeulenaere, 2020). You can attach many layers (examples, exercises, and smaller concepts) to this framework, and it neatly organizes the material in a way that participants can understand. It pedagogically groups materials.

The four levels of racism that we introduce in this course are the following:

- Internalized racism (and we incorporate discussions of horizontal racism)
- Cultural racism
- Interpersonal racism
- Institutional racism

There are, of course, more than four types of racism. I elected to focus on these four because they are accessible and generate multiple examples in the field of education. Our goal in this course is to increase participants' capacity to recognize and *see* racism in their schooling context and the field of education more broadly. Most white educators and parenting adults (and some BIPOC adults) generally enter the course with only one lens for making sense of racism in the world—interpersonal racism. This form of racism is often limited to past actions by the KKK or white people who enslaved Black people or the occasional and unfortunate actions of present-day "racists." Racism sits in the rare white person. Racism, for them initially, is not present when that rare racist person is not present. And race itself is not present unless a BIPOC person is in the room. Whiteness is not racial and white people do not have a racial identity. They just are. So there is no need to talk about or address racism unless "a racist" is present and no need to talk about race if there are no BIPOC folks present. Many BIPOC educators and parenting adults, though, feel and understand racism to be "bigger" and broader than this, but sometimes they do not have the language and theory to talk about this bigger sense of racism. For them, the four-levels framework provides language to name what they see and experience.

Our goal then is to provide multiple lenses to see the more subtle and overt ways that racism manifests:

- Internally in us all (internalized and horizontal racism)
- In our media, including curricula and textbooks (cultural racism)
- In our interpersonal relationships with others (interpersonal racism) with a focus on implicit biases (Eberhardt, 2019), microaggressions (Pierce, 1970; Solórzano & Pérez Huber, 2020; Sue, 2010), and microinterventions (Sue et al., 2020)
- In our institutional policies and practices (institutional racism)

While we do provide historical context in HTAR, we try to use many present-day examples to reinforce that racism is not only a part of our history but also a traumatic reality in the present day. Using the four levels of racism as a pedagogical framework, we define each level, provide examples of each, explore how each shows up in the course participants' contexts, and share examples of what antiracism at each level looks like.

THE TOOLS

In HTAR, we focus on teaching a number of tools to support educators and parenting adults in talking about race and taking antiracist actions in their school communities. These tools are rooted in practices from community organizing, democratic education, critical pedagogy, critical race pedagogy, and IGD.

Norms

The first tool that we teach is the use of norms. We argue that a very specific set of norms should be named and used for dialogues about race. Norms that were set for the overall school community or those set for a classroom were not designed with dialogues about race in mind, so we cannot assume that they are sufficient to hold a community through dialogues about an often-contentious topic. Since most people do not get practice talking about race growing up (and many are actively discouraged from talking about race), some participants can be "triggered" just by talking about it.

We vary the norms depending on the facilitators teaching the course and the participants enrolled in the course. One norm that all of our facilitators use is often captured as follows: "Move up and move back, centering the voices and experiences of BIPOC." Many communities will include the first part of the norm ("move up and move back"). This part of the norm asks participants to "move up" and actively contribute thoughts and ideas to the dialogue. It also asks them to strategically "move back" when necessary, remaining quiet but thoughtful so that others can contribute their thoughts and ideas. This part of the norm asks for participants to be mindful of how much airspace they take up during dialogue. The latter part of the norm ("centering the voices and experiences of BIPOC") makes this norm specific to talking about race. If we want to begin to dismantle racism in schools, then we need to make room to hear from those most adversely affected by racism.

In HTAR, we do a lot of storytelling and sharing of race stories (Magee, 2019) in class. Thus, we also include a norm to encourage confidentiality: "What's said here stays here, what's learned here leaves here." To encourage vulnerable sharing and to honor those stories shared, we ask participants not to share stories of other people when they leave class. Stories, we tell them, belong to the storyteller. They are not ours to pass on. What participants can share, though, is what they learned about themselves and about race from hearing these stories. Rather than saying, "In class today, I heard this story about . . . ," a participant might say, "Someone told a powerful story in class today and it made me think about when I . . . ." The former shares the details of someone else's story while the latter does not. Another aspect of this norm is to not bring that person's story up to the storyteller outside of class. The story was shared in a very specific context. To approach the storyteller in the teachers' lounge to ask more details about the story is to interrupt their day and ask them to perform their story on command (oftentimes in a public place). Instead, though, one might ask the storyteller if they are interested in continuing the sharing of stories and, if so, set a time and place to continue that storytelling.

Another norm that is common in our courses is to see this course as a part of a longer journey. That is, taking and completing this course is not about earning a badge of righteousness. It does not suddenly make someone no longer a part of a deeply racist structure. Excavating our own internalized racism, addressing implicit biases, learning about race theory, working against racism, and imagining racially just futures are lifelong endeavors. This course is one of many commitments to make over the course of one's life and career. This norm reminds us not to operate from a place of assumed scarcity—this is not the only class or conversation that we will have about race; there is no need to compete for airspace. It also encourages us to do this study and work with humility and appreciation; there is always more to learn, and we're never done with the journey.

And, finally, facilitators frequently include the norm "Assume positive intent; assume responsibility for impact." This norm asks the community and individuals in our community to recognize that we all come with varying degrees of knowledge and experience in talking about race. Inevitably, someone will use a word that they did not realize was offensive or share a perspective that causes someone else harm. This norm reminds our community that we are a learning space and we all came together with the best intentions of unlearning racist patterns and habits that we were socialized into and taught. We should listen to each other with this in mind. Importantly, though, this norm also asks us to make amends when it is brought to our attention that we (perhaps unintentionally) caused harm while doing this study and to work together. We must all take responsibility for the impact of our words and actions.

Mindful Listening

A second tool that we introduce in HTAR is the use of mindful listening. In past iterations of the course, we have also referred to this as expansive listening (Aguilar, 2018), resonant listening, and active listening. While each of these types of listening is unique and offers a nuanced way to be present for someone else, the underlying use of a tool that focuses on listening is to recognize that we want participants to be present for each other and listen to each other's experiences and race stories in a different way than everyday listening.

Mindful listening is listening to someone else with your entire being. It physically manifests as leaning toward the speaker. It means blocking out all other distractions. Obvious distractions include notifications on your phones (email and text messages, for example). Less obvious distractions include your own thoughts; as you listen to others, sometimes your mind strays and you begin to think about a time when that happened to you. That type of distracted listening, we refer to as "ego listening"—when you put the spotlight on yourself and filter the other person's story through your own experience: "You think that's bad, wait until you hear what happened to me. . . ."[1]

By contrast, mindful listening invites meditating on the story-teller's words, body language, and voice (is it shaky or confident or uncomfortable?). So much can be learned from a story when you listen beyond the words and morals of the story. So much can be learned about each other. Mindful listening requires putting the spotlight on the storyteller and keeping it there throughout the telling of the story. It asks that you respond with acknowledgement and appreciation rather than curiosity or critique.

Two questions come up with mindful listening. The first question is: Are all stories worthy of appreciation? What happens if the story shared is harmful? For example, what happens if a white storyteller shares a race story or experience that feels harmful to a BIPOC listener? Or what if a white participant shares a story about how "not racist" they are? Are the listeners required to show appreciation for that story? In our experience teaching HTAR, we try to place participants in racial affinity groups when we have a storytelling activity. It allows for white participants to work through their histories with racism without harming BIPOC listeners. In white affinity storytelling spaces, we try to always have a facilitator present who does both mindful listening *and* facilitator listening. Only facilitators are allowed to do facilitator listening, which involves listening for spaces where a deeper learning is possible; facilitators might note what they heard and ask a question that pushes the storyteller into deeper reflection, for example. When it is not possible to have affinity spaces for storytelling, we try to leave room for BIPOC participants to name any harm they experience as a part of the listening process. They can acknowledge what was meant to be communicated while also acknowledging how that story landed on them.

The second question that arises in mindful listening is this: Is mindful listening to stories meant to build the empathy of BIPOC for white participants? Is there any need for BIPOC to hear, learn, and empathize with white participants? In our experience, the question is less one of "need" (whether BIPOC *need* to learn to empathize with white participants) and more one of whether BIPOC are available and interested in understanding how white people are socialized into racism and white supremacy and how whiteness itself and white supremacy take hold in the internalized and interpersonal spaces of white people, white families, and white communities.

Zones: A Self-Diagnostic

The third tool that we introduce to participants in the course is a self-diagnostic tool that allows participants to be mindful of their emotional state during discussions about race. The tool in and of itself is not new or unique, and, in fact, some participants note that they use it with their own students in class (though they do not use it to talk about race). What is new to participants is the use of a self-diagnostic tool when in dialogues about race; while they recognize that discussions about race oftentimes end in ways that leave them emotionally dysregulated, they have not considered that this condition is something to address in the moment in ways other than avoidance.

The tool asks participants to consider what zone they're in throughout a dialogue about race. If they are in the safe/comfort zone (they are not experiencing an elevated heart rate, fast breathing, or any discomfort), we ask them to consider whether they are truly engaged. Are they feeling so comfortable that they don't think much about what they say and therefore don't choose their words carefully? We argue that when a person speaks from a place of deep safety/comfort, someone else will necessarily be pushed out of their comfort zone. That is, the speaker is often disrespectfully comfortable. Leonardo and Porter (2010) argue that this comfortable safe zone is only safe for some—usually white people. When they declare a space safe, they're declaring it safe for white people to say whatever they like without worry that anyone will call them racist. The argument goes, how can they be expected to do antiracist work if they're so nervous about possibly making a mistake and being called out? Yet when safe spaces are created for white people, unsafe spaces for BIPOC are necessarily created. When participants find themselves in the comfort/safe zone, we ask that they lean forward and recommit to mindful listening.

By contrast, participants might also find themselves in the danger or panic zone—when the heartbeat and breathing quicken uncomfortably and they have the urge to fight, freeze, or leave (flight). Without tools and practice talking about deeply controversial topics, participants can become panicked during a conversation about race. The zone that we encourage participants to speak from is their stretch zone—what Bell (2020) refers to as the "learning edge." The stretch zone is a place where a person is uncomfortable certainly, but not to the extent of wanting to fight, freeze, or leave. It is a productive space where learning can happen. We discuss ways to get participants from their panic zone to their stretch zone, and also have them brainstorm and share their own techniques. Some have suggested techniques such as asking for a moment to gather themselves and focusing on the breath—using mindfulness techniques.

Debate versus Dialogue

The fourth tool that we introduce is the use of dialogue. Rooted in Freirian dialogic pedagogy where the relationship among learners is nonhierarchical and committed to anti-oppressive interactions (Freire, 1970), dialogue is a way of communicating around tense and controversial topics (such as race) that centers mutual understanding and building knowledge collectively. We draw from the well-documented work of the University of Michigan in defining our class space as a dialogue (see https://igr.umich.edu/research-publications). That is, we encourage participants to engage with each other in ways that are about listening, learning, and understanding, rather than engaging with others in debates. Too often in schools when talking about race, the speakers are actually debating—trying to make sure that they win (and that their opponents lose). When K–12 educators and administrators interact in these ways with families, colleagues, and youth, schooling communities lose, as trust is diminished and young people (and their needs) are no longer centered.

In class, we engage participants in a practice debate about a low-stress topic (which are better, dogs or cats?) and ask them how they feel in their bodies during that debate (an example of this exercise can be found on our website, https://www.riseforracialjustice.org /resources, under "videos"). We then ask them to talk about the same topic (dogs or cats), but in a way where they are seeking to better understand the other person's perspective. Participants note that during debate, even about a "silly" topic like dogs versus cats, they feel tense in their bodies, and manifest behaviors similar to being in the panic zone. When the topic is higher risk—about racism in the curriculum, for example—debate can push people quickly into the panic zone and a community can be challenged to find a way to move through the conversations.

When the purpose of dialogue is rooted in antiracism work—not "feel good" work—it can profoundly change the trajectory of antiracism work in schools. If the purpose of dialogue is to make sure that everyone feels good during discussions about race, then the conversation can inadvertently become about making sure that white people are not challenged in their beliefs and that their feelings and fragility and emotionality are prioritized above racial justice. A space can only be an antiracist dialogue space when the other tools are also present and norms such as "centering the voices and experiences of BIPOC" are also used.

Racial Literacy

The final tool we introduce is racial literacy itself. In order for participants to be able to do antiracism work in schools, they have to have a basic racial literacy. As Ian Haney Lopez argued in a webinar in 2021, you cannot expect to talk to youth about race if you haven't done the work of learning about race. Compellingly, he reminds us that educators and parenting adults wouldn't teach our young people about financial health without learning about it themselves. Similarly, we cannot expect to talk about race with young people and each other if we don't have a basic, foundational understanding about race ourselves. For dialogues about race, racism, and racial justice in schools, it is critical that participants have language to have these discussions.

Racial literacy must be seen as a tool for antiracism work in schools, particularly for white people whose only view of racism is from the positionality of those who benefit from white supremacy. They need to learn about how racism plays out at the internalized, cultural, interpersonal, and institutional levels. By contrast, BIPOC often know this firsthand. For them, racial literacy is sometimes about providing language to describe what they've experienced. As schools do not teach race theory and in fact go to great lengths to tell youth that they are mistaken about how they experience race ("you're just being sensitive"), they have not had a chance to learn about how widespread what they experience is and how to name it. Racial literacy is learning how to recognize and name what they experience and giving space for them to analyze their own stories to understand the many forces at play. Too often we hear in our classes from BIPOC participants, "I thought it was just me."

ANTIRACIST PRACTICES

In addition to tools to support dialogues about race in schools and classrooms, we also teach several practices that support such dialogues. The distinction between a tool and practice is subtle and almost not worth the distinction. However, we've found that for adult learners, creating this distinction is useful to distinguish between what must always be present in dialogues about race (tools) and what is context based and goal based (antiracist practices). A tool must be ongoing and ever present in communities that are committed to antiracism. All involved agree to use the tools to make dialogue possible—to make antiracist work possible. An antiracist practice, by contrast, is what is made possible in a community committed to using the tools. It is an exercise that a group can use once or more than once.

The Power Flower

The power flower practice is a community organizing exercise with a long history. First introduced and shared in the text *Educating for a Change* (Arnold et al., 1991) and updated by many, the power flower is a visual and artistic way to explore our multiple social identities and our positionality (where we're located in the power structure due to the collection and intersection of our multiple social identities). Although there are many iterations of this visual (see the "matrix of oppression" in Adams et al., 2007), here I will share how we do this activity in HTAR.

We first take time to distinguish between personal and social identities (occasionally, depending on the group, we may also discuss role identities). We define personal identities as the identities that you choose, which are often related to habits, preferences, and hobbies. This might include identities such as athlete, gamer, introvert, artist. A role identity is an identity relevant to your location in an institution (teacher, parent, student). A social identity, though, is an identity that is associated with a system of oppression and which locates you in a power structure as a member of the targeted/oppressed/marginalized group or dominant group. Social identities include your racial, gender, class, and religious identities, for example. How much societal power you have is associated with your social identity. Important to note here is that people with marginalized identities maintain their personal and group power to act as agents in their lives and are, of course, *empowered* to act in ways that liberate their minds, spirits, and bodies. The power flower exercise is one that asks participants to identify which of their identities are associated with historical, social, and political power.

We first ask participants to draw a circle in their journals. We ask them to consider all of their social identities and to think about which ones are most salient to them. Which identities do they think about more than others? We ask them to indicate this by drawing a slice of the pie that represents how salient each identity is for them. For example, as a Black womxn, I think about race quite a bit in my day. It helps keep me safe in some respect in that I make decisions about how to handle myself if pulled over by a police officer, for example. I am often made aware of my racial identity through racial microaggressions that are directed toward me. In my power flower, I begin to create a pie chart that shows race as taking up roughly 40 percent of the pie circle. Gender, by comparison, takes up about 30 percent of my circle. I think about my identity as a cis womxn a lot because it determines, for example, how far I park from the store entrance at 9:00 P.M. when I go to grab that forgotten grocery item. Other slices that take up very little space in my power flower are citizenship, class, age, and language (see Figure 3.1).

Next, we ask participants to draw multiple petals for each slice (see Figure 3.2).

Participants then color in the inside petal (closest to the center) if they sit in the dominant group for that identity and the outer petal if they sit in the marginalized group in that identity. For race, for example, in my own power flower I shade the outer petal. As a

Figure 3.1. First step of power flower activity

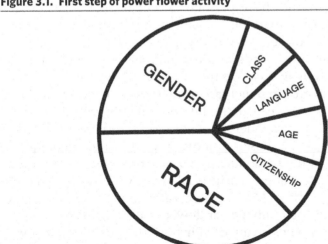

Figure 3.2. Second step of power flower activity

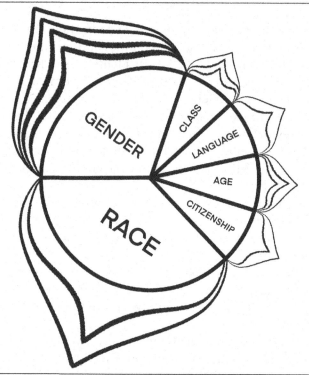

Black-identified person in a world deeply invested in anti-Black racism, racially I am a member of a racially oppressed group. This does not mean that I do not have personal power or that I do not feel empowered; it means that cultural, interpersonal, and institutional racism often target those who identify as Black. For class (socioeconomic status) identity, I shade in the middle petal. To me, the most privileged class group in society is the "1 percent." Yet I recognize that my material needs are often met (access to housing, food, and medical care) and oftentimes exceeded. So, I do not identify with those most oppressed based on class identity (low-income and working-poor adults and youth). I've chosen to locate myself in the middle petal. I've also shaded in the remaining petals based on where I fall in the power structure according to each social identity and its corresponding system of oppression. My daughter, Salihah, was kind enough to create a digital version of my power flower (see Figure 3.3).

Participants get very creative with how they draw their power flowers and shade their petals in an effort to create a power flower

Figure 3.3. Final step of power flower activity

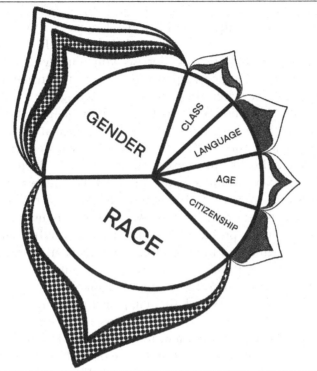

that represents the complexity of their social identities. More information about the power flower and examples of our facilitators' power flowers can be found on our website (https://www.riseforracialjustice .org/antiracistpractices).

In the debriefing, we ask participants what they notice about their flowers and what this means for how they participate in dialogues about race in schools. One thing white womxn notice often is that their race slice is very thin while their gender slice is quite wide. That is, they think about the identity where they are marginalized more so than the identity in which they are in the dominant group. We ask them then what this means about how they participate in dialogues about race. Do they notice that they try to overempathize and make comparisons to sexism when dialogues are about racism? Do they use their marginalized identities to avoid talking about race? Has the width of their race slice changed over time and, if so, why? We also often debrief with discussions about the shortcomings of this activity—such as its inability to capture experiences with intersecting oppressions.

The Inclusive Language Box

The next practice is the "the inclusive language" box. I adapted an exercise that Paul Kivel created called the "Act like a man" box (Greene, 2019). In his original exercise, you start by drawing a box on the board and asking participants to write on the inside of the box what men get called when they are seen as "acting like a man." Then on the outside of the box, they write what men get called when they are seen as not acting like a man. What they notice at the end is that the words on the outside of the box are words associated with womxn and queer folx. The ensuing conversation is rich and deep.

I took that exercise and adapted it in the following way to identify those words that we want to use when talking about racial identities and those that we do not. In class, we open by discussing how and why language can be problematic and cause harm. While language is constantly changing and there is rarely consensus on words to use in differing contexts, without it, we cannot talk about race.

We pair students up and give them a blank sheet of paper with a square box drawn on it. We ask them in pairs to determine racial iden- tity terms that they want to hear used in class and to write those words inside the box. Then we ask them to take words they never want to hear in class and write those on the outside of the box (with the added caveat that if the word is derogatory, they should write the first letter of the word and then an asterisk—we ask them *not* to write any deroga- tory words in full on their paper). Words that members of a group can call themselves, but others cannot—those words go on the line of the box. We ask them to use assigned readings as guides to the choice of words and to cite the readings. If they do not know which word should be used, they can rely on the readings provided or go to the cultural center website of a nearby university to find suggested words.

When each group is done, we draw a square on the board and start by putting the word "white" on the inside and "Caucasian" on the outside of the box. We show an episode from Francesca Ramsey's *Decoded* on the origins of the word "Caucasian" (we also sometimes use Painter [2013]) and discuss why, in class, RISE uses the term "white" instead of "Caucasian." We repeat the exercise, placing "multiracial" inside the box and "mixed" on the outside the box. We discuss the lon- ger history of efforts to "protect whiteness" (by not "mixing" blood) and, thus, property and wealth, by making sure that those with Black heritage were seen as "impure" and not worthy of whiteness because of their "mixed blood." Historically, it allowed white men who owned

Black people during enslavement to sexually violate Black womxn and ensure that her children remained enslaved (thus, creating more property for the white man) (Harris, 1993).

Each pair of participants volunteers one word on the inside of the square and one on the outside (we ask them to share terms that represent the racial identity of at least one person in the pair so that they are not "naming" another group). When a pair shares, we ask the class how they feel about that suggestion and, using our classroom norms, have a dialogue about whether we, as a community, can agree to these terms. One pair, for example, in one class, shared "Latinx/Latine" on the inside, "Hispanic" on the line, and "Spanish" (unless you are from Spain) on the outside. One person in the pair explained that their grandmother only wanted to be called Hispanic despite the history of this term and they were not going to tell their grandmother that she can't call herself what she wants to call herself. The pair also acknowledged that the term "Hispanic" is regional, more likely to be used on the East Coast than the West Coast, for example. So they wanted to allow the use of the term, but only by those who self-identified as Hispanic.

We have been asked why the term "colored people" is not the same as "People of Color" by participants for whom English is their second language. We use it as an opportunity to discuss why, even though the two terms use similar words, the first term is considered derogatory (though, as language has changed overtime, it was not always so) and the latter is not. BIPOC (Black, Indigenous, and People of Color) is a newer term that, though controversial, is also used with increasing frequency. In Figure 3.4, you will see a representative example of an inclusive language box.

Figure 3.4. Partially completed inclusive language box activity

Caucasian	white		People of Color/ BIPOC	Colored People
	Latine/x		Multiracial	
	~~Hispanic~~			
	Spanish		Mixed	

We end the discussion by checking to make sure everyone in the class concurs with what we've agreed to with the inclusive language box, and then we take a picture of that box and send it to everyone. We agree to revisit the box if anyone changes their mind or comes across new information that makes the box less relevant or current. We emphasize that language is fluid and ever changing (as the introduction of the newer term BIPOC illustrates); what we agree to as a community one day might need to change the next. We also remind them that this is an inclusive language box for *our* community. Participants cannot assume that, in a different context, the terms we agreed to hold. They should ask, in other communities, about terms that can be used in that context. Again, more information about the inclusive language box can be found on our website (https://www .riseforracialjustice.org/antiracistpractices).

The DIA Protocol and the Book Audit

Another practice that we use is the DIA protocol. DIA stands for "describe, interpret, and analyze." I developed this protocol with Diane Butler, the former Andrew W. Mellon Coordinator of Academic Affairs at the Frances Lehman Loeb Art Center at Vassar College. One aspect of her job was to work with faculty to use the college's art collection in their coursework with students. Diane and I had worked together on a number of occasions to use the collection to help make race theory more accessible to Vassar undergraduate students and to generate conversation in race theory courses. We later partnered to use the gallery collection for a workshop for K–12 educators about race.

At its core, the DIA protocol is really about building the capacity for critical media analysis—to get educators, parenting adults, and youth to look beyond an art piece's tombstone (the placard listing the title and artist) or beyond a print ad in a magazine, for example. We want participants to consider the story that the artist, producer, or author intends to tell us, how they use race to tell the story, and what, in the end, they end up teaching us about race.

In the DIA protocol, we ask participants to describe in detail what it is that they see in an art piece (print ad or other media image) that we provide. We ask them to focus on color, shading, light, and composition. Before getting into a discussion about what they think the art piece is about, we ask them to focus on what is actually there. Every aspect of the artwork or media image is intentional. DiAngelo (2012) reminds us that, in advertising, there are no mistakes. Taking the time to see the choices made reminds participants that indeed choices were made. Though they are often eager to get to the "so what?" of the analysis, taking time to really see an image allows them to find subtle choices made and wonder about those choices.

We then move into the "I" in the DIA protocol. We ask them to interpret what they see. What is the story the artist intends to tell and how is the artist using race to tell that story? The final step of the protocol is to analyze the piece—to consider what the art piece is teaching *us* about race. As we are all socialized into our understandings of race, it is important to see these pieces through the lens of pedagogy—what does the art piece (and, thus, the artist) teach or reinforce about race? For this exercise, we have used images such as the well-known Vogue magazine cover (April 2008) that features LeBron James and Gisele Bundchen (photographed by Annie Leibovitz). We look for images that we have tested with each other and vetted—images that also have sufficient complexity to generate discussion. For an example of how we use the DIA protocol, see the DIA video on our website, https://www.riseforracialjustice.org/resources under "videos."

The DIA protocol is related to another practice that we use in the HTAR course—the book audit. Similar to the DIA protocol, participants are encouraged to look at children's books using a rubric to understand how the books "talk" about and illustrate race as well as what they teach young readers about race and racism. Using the suggested book audit guide from Derman-Sparks and Ramsey (2011), we share children's books in small groups and ask the participants to consider storyline, illustrations, protagonists, and author and illustrator identity to determine whether a book belongs on a bookshelf in their room where young people can freely access it, whether it is a book that the teacher wants to read with young people (to set context or lead them through a discussion), or whether the book can be retired to make room for another book. We have reviewed books about the underground/overground railroad, books that center Black girls, books about multiracial children, and books that attempt to explicitly teach about race. We select a variety of books within each topic area for them to read.

For example, one book that we read together is *Overground Railroad*, written by Lesa Cline-Ransome and illustrated by James Ransome (2020). We show an interview of the team/couple discussing why they wrote/illustrated the book. We show Lesa reading the book, and then ask participants what they think. They use the book audit tool to think about how Black people are represented in the book (are they stereotyped? are full complex stories shared?, etc.). We ask participants to consider what makes the author/illustrator qualified to write about this topic. We ask them whether they would adopt this book for their classroom and, if so, why and how they would use it. The conversations about book audits are rigorous and energetic; educators and parenting adults appreciate this time to have these conversations.

We've also created a Black Girls Lives Matter children's book collection. This book collection features children's and young adult books about Black girls and/or Black womxn and written and/or illustrated by Black womxn authors. The physical books are housed at a Black-owned bookstore in Richmond, California, and local teachers who have completed the HTAR course can freely borrow books to use in their classrooms. We also created two guides for selecting books by and about Black girls and womxn, the Black Girls Lives Matter book list and reading guide for adults. Our goal is to not only work with educators and parenting adults on selecting books for their classrooms and homes but also to provide resources to help them find books with powerful and positive representations of Black girls and womxn—books that show the diversity and fullness of their lives.

CONCLUSION

As of the writing of this book, RISE for Racial Justice has grown to be an organization of over 15 facilitators. Each facilitator was trained as an intern in the HTAR course. Many took the course themselves and wanted to contribute back by teaching others. For many, it is their entry into a career as antiracism and racial literacy trainers.

As of June 2022, as the COVID-19 pandemic uncertainty continues, we still teach the course remotely via zoom and each facilitation team has members who are geographically spread across the country. While we use the same pedagogical framework, tools, and practices, our sections of the course differ as we each bring different experiences and pedagogical stories to share.

My goal in this chapter, though, is to share our work so that others will take what they need to grow their own communities capable of delving into dialogues about race in K–12 schools with educators and parenting adults. It's taken RISE over 5 years to create this present iteration of the HTAR course, and I expect it will continue to grow and change as new people join our team, as new forms of racial oppression emerge in schools (such as the attack on critical race theory), and as new possibilities for antiracism work arise. In the last year alone, organizations such as the Abolitionist Teaching Network, the Center of Racial Justice and Youth Engaged Research, Education for Liberation Network, Apocalyptic Education, and Making Us Matter have all increased their work in K–12 education; they have shifted the landscape, offering new ways to bring about racial justice in our schools. We are inspired by them and look forward to what they will teach us about doing this work.

NOTE

1. We'd like to offer appreciation to Jackie Heymann, who facilitated with RISE during summer 2020. She introduced the language of "spotlighting" to RISE for Racial Justice from her own training in intergroup dialogue.

REFERENCES

Adams, B. & Bell, L. A. (2016). *Teaching for diversity and social justice* (3rd ed.; D. J. Goodman & K. Y. Joshi [Eds.]). Routledge.

Adams, M., Bell, L. A., & Griffin, P. (Eds.). (2007). *Teaching for diversity and social justice* (2nd ed.). Routledge.

Aguilar, E. (2018). *Onward: Cultivating emotional resilience in educators.* Jossey-Bass.

Arnold, R., Burke, B., James, C., Martin, D., & Thomas, B. (1991). *Educating for change.* Doris Marshall Institute for Education and Action and Between the Lines.

Bell, L. A. (2020). *Storytelling for social justice: Connecting narrative and the arts in antiracist teaching.* Routledge.

Cann, C., & DeMeuleneare, E. (2020). *The activist academic: Engaged scholarship for resistance, hope, and social change.* Myers Education Press.

Cline-Ransome, L., & Ransome, J. (illustrator). (2020). *Overground railroad.* Penguin Random House.

Derman-Sparks, L., & Ramsey, P. G. (2011). *What if all the kids are white? Antibias multicultural education with young children and families.* Teachers College Press.

DiAngelo, R. (2012). How race shapes the lives of white people. *What does it mean to be white? Developing white racial literacy* (pp. 133–165). Peter Lang.

Eberhardt, J. (2019). *Biased: Uncovering the hidden prejudice that shapes what we see, think, and do.* Viking.

Freire, P. (1970). *Pedagogy of the oppressed*. Continuum Publishing.

Greene, M. (2019). *The history of "The Man Box."* Retrieved March 27, 2022, from https://paulkivel.com/resource/origins-of-the-act-like-a-man-box.

Haney Lopez, I. (2021, January 18). *Ian López on what it means to be white, a race and power conversation*. Leadership for society: Race and power series. Stanford Graduate School of Business. Accessed on January 10, 2022, from https://gsb-courses.stanford.edu/leadership-for-society/race-and-power-winter-2021.

Leonardo, Z., & Porter, R. K. (2010). Pedagogy of fear: Topward a Fanonian theory of "safety" in race dialogue. *Race Ethnicity and Education, 13*(10), 139–157.

Magee, R. (2019). *The inner work of racial justice: Healing ourselves and transforming our communities through mindfulness*. TarcherPerigee.

Painter, N. (2013). *Why White People Are Called 'Caucasian'* (Lecture). Berkeley Graduate Lectures. https://gradlectures.berkeley.edu/lecture/caucasian.

Pierce, C. (1970). Offensive mechanisms. In F. B. Barbour (Ed.), *The Black seventies* (pp. 265–282). Porter Sargent Publisher.

Solórzano, D. G., & Pérez Huber, L. (2020). *Racial microaggressions: Using critical race theory to respond to everyday racism*. Teachers College Press.

Sue, D. W. (2010). *Microaggressions in everyday life: Race, gender, and sexual orientation*. Wiley.

Sue, D. W, Calle, C. Z., Mendez, N., Alsaidi, S., & Glaeset, E. (2020). *Microintervention strategies: What you can do to disarm and dismantle individual and systemic racism*. Wiley.

Tatum, B. D. (1997/2017). *Why are all the Black kids sitting together in the cafeteria?: And other conversations about race*. Basic Books.

CHAPTER 4

The Practicality of the Seemingly Impractical

Why We Have a Course on Race Theory

Colette N. Cann

RISE for Racial Justice offers several intermediate-level courses to build on the learning of those who completed How to Talk About Race (HTAR). The first intermediate course was designed in response to several requests from educators who were yearning for more ways to remain engaged in learning about race, racism, and racial justice in schools. With the help of Robin Alpern, who co-taught the first iteration of the course with me, I designed a course on race theory that built on what educators had learned in HTAR and introduced them more deeply to critical race theory (CRT). This chapter discusses why the decision was made to offer a course on race theory and why theory is critical for K–12 educators. The chapter also shares the curriculum and classroom activities used in this course.

WHY RACE THEORY?

Tatum (1997/2017), in her seminal text *Why Are All the Black Kids Sitting Together in the Cafeteria?*, discusses how important theory (and, in her text, she refers specifically to racial identity development theory) is to the work of educators. Without access to theory, she writes, "educators all across the country, most of whom are White, are teaching in racially mixed classrooms, daily observing identity development in process, and are without an important interpretive framework to help them understand what is happening in their interactions with students, or even in their cross-racial interactions with colleagues" (2017, p. 75).

This "interpretive framework" provided by race theory helps educators and parenting adults make sense of their racialized worlds and contexts. Without this theory, we are at the mercy of dominant ideologies—most of which rely on explanations that blame individuals for their successes or failures—to explain injustice.

Race theory takes the focus off blaming individuals. Ideologies like meritocracy seek to have us believe that people who have the resources to meet their needs (and those with excess of those very resources) have earned what they have through their own hard work. And those without those same means have not worked hard enough to be deserving of health care, housing, food, and wellness. Those in lower tracked classes, lower income neighborhoods, and the working poor, according to this ideology, deserve the lives they lead because, at some earlier point, they made a choice to not work hard enough to pull themselves up by their own bootstraps. Such explanations, of course, fail to acknowledge the role of generational wealth rooted in exploitative economic systems of racial capitalism, systems rooted in violent settler colonialism and anti-Black racism.

People of Color come to believe these ideologies just as white people do. They internalize these ideologies and the narratives and stereotypes that support them. These ideologies have been at play for centuries and have justified enslavement and land theft and justify current technologies of racial oppression in the form of, to name two, the school-to-prison pipeline (harsh disciplinary measures that target Youth of Color) and the prison industrial complex (the creation of policies that target Populations of Color, oversurveil them, increase punishment sentences, and make it challenging to escape the system).

The Pane of Glass

We all walk through the world holding a pane of glass in front of us. We see an event through that pane of glass. That pane of glass has undulations and tints and cracks that result from our life experiences. Thus, no two people have identical panes of glass. When I see a Black person pulled over on the side of the road by a police officer, I see that through my unique pane of glass. The undulations are created by my own experiences as a Black womxn in the world. It is tinted by my experiences of being pulled over for speeding on a highway when others were passing me in the fast lane; by the officer who pulled my car over with myself, my daughter, and a Black student who we were driving to the airport—pulled us over onto a tiny side road where we could not be seen by passing cars; by the officer throwing my license back at me when I attempted to pass it to him through the window. My window pane is chipped by my experience as a 5-year-old watching my father be pulled over as we drove through Texas, for allegedly speeding—though we were in the slow lane being passed by other cars; watching my father plead to allow him to follow them to the police station rather than having them take him in a police car and having social services come get me and my sister (he had an out-of-state license, which set in motion a set of regulations); watching him plead again to be held in the office where we could see him through a glass window rather than in a cell downstairs; all while waiting for our grandfather to come post bail. My glass pane is coated with a haze of dust left by the officer who pulled me over while walking down the street in Palo Alto to my car; by his decision to pull into a driveway to cut off my path down the sidewalk; by his question, "What are you doing here (in Palo Alto)?"; by his rationale that he pulled me over because I (a Black womxn) looked (stereotypically) mad (because a truck full of men had just catcalled me and I had been engaged in giving them the finger along with other colorful words); by my asking for his badge number and telling him that I was going to the police department to report him and his calm response, "I'll just tell them that I pulled you over because you meet the description on an APB of a Black man wearing a green t-shirt." Then he smiled. I wasn't wearing a green t-shirt. My glass pane is tinted by the on-campus officer who stopped me while pushing my daughter in a stroller as we were walking the dog around the campus of our new home—we had just moved there for a new tenure-track position I'd accepted. "What are you doing here?" he asked. "I live here," I replied. So, when I see a Black person pulled over to the side of the road, I see that through this pane of glass informed by my own past experiences. I know that being pulled over "while Black", whether while driving or walking, is real and can result in the unjust and tragic death of Black people.

The Polarizing Filter

Solórzano (2013) describes race theory as a polarizing filter on a camera lens. When we aim a camera at a shop window to take a picture, it will often only capture our own reflection in that window. Yet, when we add a filter, sometimes that filter will allow the camera to penetrate beyond the glare on the window to capture what is inside the shop. That filter, Solórzano says, is theory—a tool that allows us to see what has always been there, but that we did not have the tools to be able to see, understand, or make sense of without the filter—without the theory. Solórzano describes theory as follows:

> As a researcher, a theory is a lens through which we observe and interpret social life. That's what theory is. . . . That's how I use the tool of theory. It helps me interpret social phenomena. A theory often comes to mind to explain what it is I'm seeing. . . . As you use a critical race lens, race and racism come into focus because they are central to the analysis.

A "Getting-Free"

Theory, and race theory specifically, is a promise of change and liberation. It is the promise of *personal* change and societal liberation—a "getting-free" from dominant narratives that can make BIPOC believe that we are less than we are and make white people believe that they are more than BIPOC. It can be a getting-free from narratives that make us control ourselves and limit ourselves in ways that benefit those in power. Race theory helps us make sense of structures larger than ourselves and sets the stage for praxis (Freire, 1970)—those moments when reflection begets action begets more reflection and, thus, the potential for real significant change.

WHAT WE TALK ABOUT IN CLASS

I started teaching the Race Theory course in 2018 with Robin Alpern. Graduates of HTAR wanted to learn more about race theory. They had been excited to learn about different levels of racism and found that pedagogical framework helped them make sense of what was happening in their classrooms, in their schools, and in their lives. At the time, I was teaching an undergraduate course on race theory, and Robin and I decided to redesign it for K–12 educators in the form of a 6-week course. In the first iteration of the course, Robin and I identified six topics from the undergraduate race theory course that would provide important polarizing filters through which to better see how race and racism are invoked in educational spaces. These six topics included racial identity development, intersectionality, construction of race/racism, whiteness, counterstorytelling, and interest convergence.

Although the undergraduate course was 37.5 hours, we only had 18 hours in the 6-week course for K–12 educators,. Educators took the class at the end of a busy work week at the end of a busy workday. Some of them were also parenting young children. The time that they could put toward reading and writing before class was limited. Yet they brought decades of experience in the field of education, as well as race stories informed by living in different political, geographical, and professional contexts. We had rich and rigorous conversations in the classroom.

Introducing the Course

In the first course meeting, we spend time re-creating a sense of community (setting norms, reminding participants about the use of mindful listening, dialogue, and the self-diagnostic zones tool; see Chapter 3). Participants in the intermediate course come from across several different sections of HTAR and often only know a few people initially. So, we spend the first session setting up this new community to work together and engage in difficult conversations about race.

At this first meeting, we also provide a brief review of our conversations from HTAR. We reinforce that they've already begun the study of CRT in that course by studying the four levels of racism (see Chapter 3). That is, one of the core tenets of CRT is that racism is endemic and everyday. Racism, in fact, grows here in the United States, for example, as a plant grows in an environment that meets its every need. It shows up in our everyday lives, and the study of the four levels of racism is one way of sharpening our ability to see and understand the ways that racism is not an exception, but the rule.

We remind the participants that racism cannot be contained by the interpersonal space. It, in fact, overflows despite our best efforts to shove it untidily onto that one overtly racist person we know. Racism, in fact, is built into the foundations of our society and manifests in the ways we are socialized to see ourselves and others, in the images that are so pervasive in media (including our curricula), and institutionally in our policies, institutional culture, and even in how we move through these institutions. And, of course, these forms of racism intersect, interact, are mutually dependent, and magnify each other's effects. Structural racism is the smooth, well-oiled teamwork of institutions reinforcing the wellness of whiteness and white people and the ongoing (legalized and justified) oppression of People of Color.

We also spend the first class session letting participants know that the Race Theory course is very different from HTAR. While we do introduce some race theory in the introductory course—namely, we focus on introducing four levels of racism (internalized, cultural, interpersonal, and institutional)—we also introduce tools and practices that allow them to talk about, interrogate, and make sense of race and racism with colleagues, families, and youth. Our focus is indeed on giving them skills and practice to talk about race. In the Race Theory course, though, we are less concerned with learning practical skills to talk about race and more concerned about gaining new polarizing filters to use in our lives and work.

The Race Theory course was particularly important in summer 2021. CRT was under attack, and educators who teach about race in K–12 schools were seen as either liars changing history to frame white people as guilty or reverse racists targeting white people for crimes not committed. Educators were, in some states, prevented from teaching about race and Diversity, Equity, and Inclusion (DEI) groups prevented from meeting. A number of educators came to this course because they needed a space to process and make sense of this attack on CRT.

Though Robin no longer coteaches this course, we continue to offer it. I now coteach it with graduate students in the Racial Justice in Education doctoral program at the University of San Francisco. These are students who have taken a course in CRT, a course in whiteness, and two ethnic studies courses of their choice. The course is still taught to K–12 educators, but now also includes parenting adults and others interested in a course on race theory. Participants need HTAR as a prerequisite. The course is also now taught remotely due to the ongoing COVID-19 pandemic. In the latest iteration of the course, we include the following topics: racial identity development, intersectionality, racial capitalism, whiteness as privilege, supremacist culture, and property and interest convergence. I will share in more detail these topics below.

Exploring the Content

Racial Identity Development. The first theory that we discuss is racial identity development. We assign readings that look at the racial identity of different racial (or racialized) groups, and participants select the set of readings that feels most relevant to how they identify racially. Prior to reading, we ask them to create a journey line of their own racial identity development. Specifically, we ask them to think about how they understand and define race and racism and how they thought about their own racial identity at five points in time: in elementary school, middle school, high school, and college/post–high school, and as educators now. Thus, we ask them to describe the shape of their pane of glass prior to reading about the polarizing filter, racial identity development. Once they've completed their journey line and completed the readings, we ask them to then create an artistic piece using the medium of their choice to share their own racial identity development (using both notes from their journey line and from the reading).

Some examples of artistic pieces that have been created include interpretive dance, digital and paper collage, paintings, music, and poems. At our next class meeting, they share their artwork in racial affinity spaces. These are always powerful and emotional sessions. For many, this is the first time they've used art to express their own thinking about race, racism, and racial identity. Below, I've included two examples of my own artistic responses to the assignment (facilitators also complete the art project); as I've done this art project multiple times, I have many iterations of my artist racial identity development journey (see Figure 4.1 and Figure 4.2). Each of the drawings represents six distinct moments in my racial identity development journey (I attended two high schools, and so I have two different representations for high school). I explain in my racial affinity space why I selected the images that I did and what they mean in terms of how I understood race and what my own racial identity meant to me at that time.

Figure 4.1. One of my artistic representations of my racial identity development journey

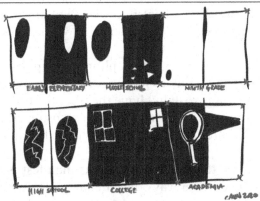

**Figure 4.2. Another of my artistic representations of my racial identity
        development journey**

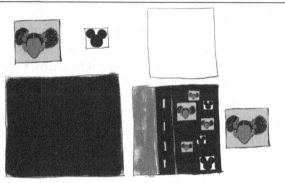

At the end of the session, facilitators conduct a minilecture on racial identity development (drawing from their assigned readings), visually summarizing racial identity development models (and a more general social identity development model [Adams, 2016]).

Intersectionality. We next discuss intersectionality, a term coined by Kimberlé Crenshaw (1989) in an article she wrote called "Demarginalizing the Intersection of Race and Sex" in 1989. Crenshaw (1991) continued to write about intersectionality in her seminal article, "Mapping the Margins." She defines intersectionality as follows:

> The various ways in which race and gender interact to share the multiple dimensions of Black women's . . . experiences. . . . The intersection of racism and sexism factors into Black women's lives in ways that cannot be captured wholly by looking at the race or gender dimensions of those experiences separately. [Their intersection shapes] structural, political, and representations aspects of [the experiences of] women of color. (p. 1244)

Referencing Solórzano's (2013) metaphor of the polarizing filter, we discuss how intersectionality as race theory allows us to see what has always been there, but we didn't have the filter to be able to acknowledge, make sense of, and understand. That is, using an intersectional analytical lens, we are better able to understand how Black womxn stand at the intersection of racial and gender-based oppressions, and yet the unique way that these oppressions manifest is often unseen and unacknowledged. The ways that the law defined harm excluded the ways that harm is experienced by Womxn of Color. They are differently vulnerable before the courts, in media and in interpersonal relationships. Often excluded from racial justice and gender-justice movements, Black womxn are also unseen in calls for change.

In class, we conduct a critical media analysis of the ways in which Anita Hill, Christine Blasey Ford, Brett Kavanaugh, and (mostly recently added) Ketanji Brown Jackson were interviewed during Supreme Court confirmation hearings—how they were differently questioned and how they were differently allowed to present themselves in order to be received as credible. We then ask participants to consider how using an intersectional lens helps us see the experiences of Trans and Cis-girls of Color in schools differently. What comes into view or focus when an intersectional polarizing filter is added to their camera lens? How are policies designed to overlook or not acknowledge as credible the ways that they experience harm?

We close the session asking them to consider how theory might be useful to their work. Specifically, we ask, "How might you take an intersectional lens back to your workplace to see what you might be overlooking? How might it help you see stereotypes and single narratives that allow schools to blame students affected by intersecting oppressions?"

Racial Capitalism. When introducing racial capitalism, we start with Cedric Robinson's *Black Marxism* (1983). We discuss how and why racism preceded capitalism. While we tend to think of racism as starting with the racial oppression of Black people, Europe used the differentiation of Irish, Jewish, Roma, and Slavic people to exploit them using racialism to dispossess, enclose, and colonize people within Europe. Racial capitalism is not a type of capitalism, since there is no such thing as a nonracial capitalism. Capitalism begins with seizing natural resources and using cheap or free labor to create profit. Yet land and labor cannot be seized without racial violence, and it cannot be maintained without ongoing racial violence. In addition to Robinson, we also consider the work of Ruth Gilmore (we share her video *Geographies of Racial Capitalism with Ruth Wilson Gilmore* [Card, 2020]) and Nancy Leong's (2013) seminal piece on racial capitalism. When discussing the work of each of these scholars, we show their pictures and use direct quotes from their work. Our goal is to make theorists relatable and feel accessible and relevant to the work of educators.

We end the class meeting by watching the 30-minute "Space Traders" segment of the television anthology movie *Cosmic Slop* (Hudlin, 1994), an adaption of Derrick Bell's counterstory of the same name

(Bell, 1992). In this movie, aliens from outer space arrive on Earth to ask the U.S. president for all of the Black people in the country. In exchange for all of the Black people, the Space Traders will eradicate the national debt and clean the environment of pollutants. The question the movie raises is whether the country (via a referendum) is willing to sacrifice the health and wellness of Black people for its own (white) self-interest.

After the movie, we ask participants to consider what it felt like to watch this movie in an interracial group and what feelings came up for them as they watched. We also debrief the movie by asking them:

- What examples of racial capitalism did you observe in the film?
- What did you learn from this film?
- How was this race story important for your learning?
- What are the pedagogical possibilities of this type of storytelling?

Whiteness. On our fifth day, we discuss whiteness. Our hope is that we have built enough community to engage in a direct conversation about a topic that is often invisible in discussions about race. When it is discussed, we often limit our discussion to addressing white *people*, which then obscures whiteness as privilege, white supremacy culture, and whiteness as property. What goes unnamed is whiteness as a construct created to oppress People of Color and justify the theft of land, labor, and lives.

Prior to this class session, participants read a shortened version of Cheryl Harris's seminal article "Whiteness as Property" (Harris, 1995). She opens this article with a poem written for and about her grandmother, a woman who raised her children alone. As a Black womxn, many jobs that paid enough to support her family were closed to her. She, instead, risked her life by passing as white to secure a position that would allow her to financially support her children. Harris' grandmother shared stories of her journeys across the color line with Harris, prompting Harris to write a poem called "Poem for Alma." In this poem, Harris introduces the idea of a racial hierarchy as normalized, as legalized, as violent. In this poem, of which we only get five lines, we see that this racial hierarchy is the difference between life and death. It is present in our personal, public, and legal lives.

We open this class session asking participants to also merge art with race theory. We ask them to pen their own five-line poem that captures the role that whiteness played in the life of a significant elder or ancestor. We ask them to take a moment to think of this loved one and consider how whiteness showed up in a way that mattered. Below is the poem that I shared about a beloved ancestor in my life.

> It kept him from achieving his dreams.
> For he defined those dreams by success in their world.
> And when the gates to their world were closed,
> He found that he did not have the key
> To the only lock that mattered to him.

These poems create a space at the opening of this class that is personal and yet points to structure—points to something more than interpersonal racism.

We then introduce whiteness as a construct. Referencing the census, we ask them to consider how the racial identity terms have changed over time. The terms used to describe Black people, for example, shifted from a labeling that indicated their status as enslaved or free to labels that indicate racial identity such as African American and Black. We also call attention to the fact that the most stable racial category in the census across all racial groups is the category defining white people.

We then look at whiteness through three different lenses. We look at white as privilege, white supremacy culture, and whiteness as property. We start with whiteness as privilege, introducing them to the work of McIntosh (1990) because, for most, they've heard of the concept of white privilege even if they've never heard of Peggy McIntosh. It is accessible and begins to introduce subtle ways that white people move through the world with what we term interpersonal and institutional "micro-uplifts"—confirmations and affirmations that they are the norm, they represent right ways of being, and they are deservedly superior. (Micro-uplifts are what white people experience when stereotypes of white people as superior provide advantage; while BIPOC experience racial microaggressions, white people experience racial micro-uplifts. We draw from the work of Walton and Cohen (2003), who found that white students experience "stereotype uplift" when performing on "intellectual tests." They define stereotype uplift as "the performance boost caused by the awareness that a [racial] outgroup is negatively stereotyped" (p. 456). Knowing that BIPOC are stereotyped as inferior intellectually, white test takers perform better.) McIntosh's seminal article includes a list of ways in which the world has been created to affirm her as a white person. She refers to this as her invisible knapsack. In this knapsack are privileges such as the ability to be late without having it attributed to her race, or shopping for hair supplies at any store and being able to find what she needs.

This article and way of codifying whiteness as a list of invisible privileges has been critiqued by Leonardo (2004) as only touching the surface of white supremacy. McIntosh does not list the ways white supremacy operates through laws and how, at a structural level, BIPOC are locked out of opportunities that create wellness and wealth. For example, she does not mention histories of redlining, compulsory ignorance laws, black codes, or racial terror like lynching and state-sanctioned violence against Communities of Color. Without this more complete understanding of white supremacy, we are left with an incomplete and insufficient understanding of what whiteness is.

We also introduce participants to white supremacy culture and the work of Okun (2021), who recently relaunched a website on dismantling white supremacy culture. We add culture to our study because of its power to influence and determine without actually being seen or understood. Then we circle back to Harris (1995) and discuss what she means by whiteness as property. Historically, of course, racial capitalism evolved in the United States to create Black people as property. Black people themselves became what white people, even indentured servants, could not become. Poor white people with no power and no means had at least one thing—their whiteness, which prevented the possibility of lifelong enslavement. Black bodies could be bought and sold, stand in for debt, and otherwise generate wealth for white people. Over time, though, Harris argues that whiteness itself became property (though it does not always consistently follow the legal expectations of what constitutes property).

Our final assignment in the class is to create an artistic piece that captures how participants define, understand, and make sense of whiteness. They have roughly 30 minutes of class time to conceptualize this and then the week to complete it. They present it at the next class session during a gallery walk. Participants in the past have created collages, poems, and paintings. One such poem, "The United States of Karens" (Cleveland, 2020), was published and shared on Northern Public Radio. And, below, I also include an example of my own artistic response to this prompt, titled, "Shades of Whiteness: A Pale Tale" (see Figure 4.3).

Interest Convergence. We end the course with the study of Bell's (1987) concept of interest convergence (see Chapter 1). We also share

Figure 4.3. "Shades of Whiteness: A Pale Tale" by Colette Cann

the work of Dudziak (2009), again showing the pictures of Bell and Dudziak and pulling the major arguments from their pieces to share. We then focus on how participants themselves see examples of interest convergence in the field of education, in their districts, in their schools, and even in their own work with youth in their classrooms. We focus in this last session on giving them time to talk about how the theory of interest convergence helps them see what they might not have otherwise been able to see without this polarizing filter.

As it is the last day of the course, we spend half of our time looking at this concept and the other half reflecting more broadly on the question of why educators and parenting adults should study race theory. How is it useful? We end with the broader discussion of how the theory they studied over the 6 weeks helps them see anew.

HUMANIZING INSTRUCTION DURING MULTIPLE PANDEMICS

As this iteration of the Race Theory course was taught during the COVID-19 pandemic and amid ongoing environmental and racism pandemics, we designed a reading assignment schedule that would allow participants to balance their work-life-wellness responsibilities. It was our intention to recognize that all of us were contending with different challenges and to support participants in approaching study in healthy ways. We offered three options for *how* to read. We asked them to consider how they were feeling on a scale of 0 to 10:

- 7–10 meant they were feeling relatively well-resourced in terms of time and energy. They had enough to give to themselves and to others. They had time and energy (and excitement) to read deeply. For this group, we provided lots of readings from which to pick and choose.
- 4–6 meant they were feeling that they had just enough resources for themselves (or for others like family or students)—but certainly not enough time and energy for both. For participants in this category, we wanted them to read, but we also wanted them to take time for themselves for radical self-care (using time to go for a walk, meditate, make a meal, or spend time with loved ones, for example).
- 1–3 meant they were without the resources that they needed to feel well physically, emotionally, and mentally. We asked participants in this group to reach out for support from family, loved ones, or a medical professional so that they could get needed support. If this was the case, we asked that they simply use the week to take care of themselves.

We made sure that at every session there were opportunities for direct instruction—what we called minilectures—to cover core concepts from the readings, introduce the participants to the theorists, and share direct quotes from the theorists' work. Thus, even those who did not have the personal resources to read that week could participate in the co-construction of knowledge at our class sessions.

We also offered remote office hours every other week for those who missed class to catch up. Having office hours reinforced the importance of the dialogue about the material while introducing enough flexibility to miss class as needed. More often than not, though, participants came to office hours to discuss what was happening in their own local sites or to do more personal reflection. Typically, 1–3 participants showed up for office hours and we met as a large group to learn more about their work and life contexts.

CONCLUSION

Race theory, I believe, saves lives. It, in a very real way, continues to save mine. To have access to polarizing filters to make sense of race and racism in a world intent on your destruction is to have access to tools to counter racial battle fatigue. Race theory is the minister in the F.A.M.E. church on a Sunday morning and the "Amens" from the congregation are the exciting beats of my heart when I have an "aha" moment when reading new race theory. I remember when I first read bell hooks, Derrick Bell, Gloria Ladson-Billings, Daniel Solórzano, Tara Yosso, William Smith, Kimberlé Crenshaw, Mari Matsuda, adrienne maree brown, Richard Delgado, Charles Mills, Zeus Leonardo, Dolores Delgado Bernal, David Stovall, and others just as I remember other important moments in my life. There is an intimacy, honesty, and power to race theory that speaks caringly to those quiet whispers planted by long histories of racism. I am grateful for these offerings and hope that those introduced to race theory in our intermediate class are similarly healed.

REFERENCES

Bell, D. (1987). *And we are not saved: The elusive quest for racial justice*. Basic Books.

Bell, D. (1992). The Space Traders (chapter). *Faces at the bottom of the well: The permanence of racism* (pp. 158–194). Basic Books.

Card, K. (Director). (2020). *Geographies of racial capitalism with Ruth Wilson Gilmore*. Antipode Foundation.

Cleveland, H. (2020). The United States of Karens. Accessed on January 10, 2022, from https://www.northernpublicradio.org/arts/2020-12-11 /poetically-yours-ep-19-california-poet-shares-her-interpretation-of -white-privilege.

Crenshaw, K. (1989). Demarginalizing the intersection of race and sex: A Black feminist critique of antidiscrimination doctrine, feminist theory and antiracist politics. *University of Chicago Legal Forum, 1989*(1:8), 139–167.

Crenshaw, K. (1991). Mapping the margins: Intersectionality, identity politics, and violence against women of color. *Stanford Law Review, 43*(6), 1241–1300.

Dudziak, M. L. (2009). Desegregation as a cold war imperative. In E. Taylor, D. Gillborn, & G. Ladson-Billings (Eds.), *Foundations of critical race theory in education*. Routledge.

Freire, P. (1970). *Pedagogy of the oppressed*. Continuum Publishing.

Harris, C. (1995). Whiteness as property. In K. Crenshaw, N. Gotanda, G. Peller, & K. Thomas (Eds.), *Critical race theory: The key writings that formed the movement* (pp. 276–291). The New Press.

Harris, C. I. (1993). Whiteness as property. *Harvard Law Review, 106*(8), 1707–1791.

Hudlin, R. (Director). (1994). Segment Space traders. *Cosmic Slop*.

Leonardo, Z. (2004). The color of supremacy: Beyond the discourse of 'white privilege.' *Educational Philosophy and Theory, 36*(2), 137–152.

Leong, N. (2013). Racial capitalism. *Harvard Law Review, 126*(8), 2151–2226.

McIntosh, P. (1990). White privilege: Unpacking the invisible knapsack. *Independent School, 49*(2), 31–36.

Okun, T. (2021). (Divorcing) white supremacy culture: Coming home to who we really are. Accessed on January 10, 2022, from https://www.whitesupremacyculture.info.

Robinson, C. J. (1983). *Black marxism: The making of the Black radical tradition*. Zed Press.

Solórzano, D. G. (2013). *Critical race theory, part I*. St. Mary's College. Accessed on January 10, 2022, from https://www.youtube.com/watch?v=iti9NUDrFd8.

Tatum, B. D. (1997/2017). *Why are all the Black kids sitting together in the cafeteria?: And other conversations about race*. Basic Books.

Walton, G. M., & Cohen, G. L. (2003). Stereotype lift. *Journal of Experimental Social Psychology, 39*, 456–467.

CHAPTER 5

Developing a Community of Reflective Practice

Ongoing Support for Those Who Complete HTAR

Brett Collins and Masumi Hayashi-Smith

In this chapter, we describe a course that we created to support participants who took How to Talk About Race (HTAR), the introductory course of RISE for Racial Justice, and want to join a community of educators and parenting adults who are taking actions in their schooling communities but need support. Our course is called How to Talk About Race: A Community of Reflective Practice (CORP). In CORP, we create an intimate space in which 5–7 participants can review and deepen their understanding of the four levels of racism introduced in HTAR (see Chapter 3) while also layering in principles of reflective practice (Finlay, 2008), social justice ecosystems (Iyer, 2020), and the cycles of socialization and liberation (Harro, 2000). Our goal for CORP is to build competence and confidence as participants take antiracist action into their personal and professional lives.

OUR JOURNEYS IN RACIAL JUSTICE FACILITATION

Brett (she/her)

I am a social worker, educator, and mother who grew up on occupied Ohlone land, also known as San Francisco, CA. I typically identify as white; that is how I am most racialized and that is the privilege I consistently receive. However, I have recently started to also identify as a Gringa-Latina due to an evolving awareness of the many ways in which my Latinx/e heritage has been erased via white supremacy. I joined RISE for Racial Justice as a facilitator for HTAR and have had the joy of creating the HTAR CORP with Masumi Hayashi-Smith.

I owe the major milestones in my formal antiracism journey to Drs. Colette Cann, Allison Briscoe-Smith, and Jessica Daniel. In addition, I give thanks to Dawn Belkin-Martinez and Dr. Joanna Herrera for instilling in me the tools of narrative therapy and reflective practice. Now, as an educational facilitator and program director at San Francisco State University, I call on the wisdom and steadfastness of these womxn to advocate for equity and liberation in education.

Just as influential in my antiracist training are the relationships that taught me about power and privilege in "the real world." Thank you to the youth I served who were persistent when I was resistant to learning about who I am and how I show up. Thank you to my own children and the "unschooling community" for requiring that I practice what I preach. And thank you to the families involved with the child welfare, mental health, and juvenile "justice" systems who taught me that abolitionism takes many forms.

Masumi (they/she)

I am a biracial music educator and facilitator who grew up on occupied Coast Salish and Puyallup land in Tacoma, WA. I owe so much of my personal growth and ability to talk about systems of oppression to an undergraduate BIPOC student program at Brown University known as the "Third World Transition Program." Participating in the program as a first-year student brought some of my most transformative friendships and helped me understand my relationship to systems of power based on race, gender, class, ability, and empire. In the next 3 years, I was able to help lead the program and, in the process, learned a lot about facilitation and organizing.

During and after college, I spent time in Sri Lanka, where I first researched an intergroup dialogue (IGD) program between Tamil and Sinhala youth. Later, I researched the ways that educators taught about history, and how those narratives contributed to or disrupted people's relationships to the protracted war. In particular, I was interested in how oppressed populations are pressured by governments to teach histories that dehumanize them, and how they resist this effort at dehumanization.

After spending a few years as an elementary music teacher, I was fortunate to meet Dr. Colette Cann. Through connecting with RISE for Racial Justice, I returned to work as an antiracism facilitator, and had the joy and privilege of collaborating with Brett Collins in creating CORP.

A DESCRIPTION OF THE COURSE AND
RATIONALE FOR THE COURSE DESIGN

We created CORP when we felt there was a need for HTAR participants to continue the work of processing and integrating what they learned in the introductory 6-week course. Participants receive a lot of information in HTAR. While it is a very interactive experience, we also knew that people were yearning to dialogue even more with each other to deepen their relationship to the material. We wanted to give them a space to process what they had learned, apply it, and have community as they move into action. Participants create action plans at the end of HTAR, and then come to CORP for accountability and critical reflection as they move their plans into action.

CORP classes run for six 2-hour sessions. The structure varies based on the group composition and the needs of participants. In general, each session starts with grounding and acknowledgements for Indigenous rights and Black Lives Matter, includes a focus on one of the levels of racism explored through small and large group dialogue, and finishes with opportunities for individual participants to share their current racial justice work and to receive support from the community of practice. While we continue to rely on some of the core tools from HTAR (e.g., norms, mindful listening, racial literacy; see Chapter 3), the primary focus in CORP is on dialogue, somatic practices, and reflective practices, which we discuss in turn below.

Dialogue

We chose a dialogue model for CORP because it most effectively facilitates interactive learning (see Chapters 2 and 3). Often, we use the metaphors of "chewing on" or "digesting" to describe what happens in CORP. We also dedicate time to different configurations of dialogic space so that everyone can interact at a level that best matches their learning style. We have opportunities to talk within the larger group, spaces to connect in small subgroups, and also spaces organized by racial affinity. Each space creates different opportunities for people to share.

Having an interactive dialogue–based community of practice creates a stronger sense of accountability for participants. There is less of an ability to be quietly passive because everyone knows that the facilitators are interested in what they have to say. Furthermore, it creates a culture in which all participants show interest in each other and an expectation to learn about each person's perspective and experience—including their experiences attempting to put racial justice into practice. Using a "brave space" approach (Arao & Clemens, 2013), we encourage participants to lean into discomfort in order to grow and connect as a community.

Somatics

In addition to leaning into dialogic practices, we also encourage participants to somatically connect to the material. Inspired by the work of Magee (2019) and other Black mindfulness practitioners, every session starts with a grounding exercise, and we regularly check in with participants about how the concepts and conversation topics feel in their body. For example, people might notice their shoulders rising when talking about a stressful situation, or that they feel physical discomfort when confronting a new part of themselves. We encourage participants to regularly pause and take a breath as well as focus on the ways that their body is physically responding to the emotions they feel.

Reflective Practice

In addition to the core tools from HTAR, in CORP we add more formal reflective practices. While the art of reflectivity takes on many names, we drew inspiration from the work of Schön (1983) and Dewey (1966 [1859–1952]) and from Brett's clinical experience (see Heffron & Murch, 2010) to use the term "reflective practice." Just as reflectivity has many names, it also can have many definitions. As facilitators, we share with participants Finlay's (2008) definition of reflective practice as "learning through and from experience towards gaining new insights of self and/or practice" with the aim of "examining assumptions of everyday practice" and "critically evaluating [practitioners'] own responses to practice situations" (p. 1).

In our own process as facilitators, we have come to appreciate these three tools—dialogue, somatics, and reflective practice—in supporting participants to (1) find a deeper sense of agency in racial justice, regardless of their starting point, (2) take informed action in a variety of settings, and (3) support each other as community members. In the most current iteration of CORP, we rely on the group to guide when and where we highlight or emphasize these tools and to what degree.

CRITICAL MOMENTS OF CHALLENGE

As facilitators, there are several tensions we face and hold in the space of CORP. Like many race-related dialogue spaces, we experience the following facilitating challenges in CORP:

- Balancing dialogue with information giving/didactic work
- Keeping the focus on race (versus other forms of oppression)
- Fostering personal introspection over theoretical discussion or the actions of others
- Promoting tangible change while being mindful of action bias

As CORP has fewer participants than other RISE for Racial Justice courses, we can be more flexible, and can manage these situations in real time through transparent conversation between the facilitators and the entire group. For example, the facilitators might notice participants having difficulty answering a reflective prompt and can pause the discussion or activity to name their observations and ask for the group's insight or suggestions on how to proceed. Through this process, the group will lead us in directions we weren't expecting. For example, on one occasion, we realized that we needed to review definitions or concepts from HTAR so that the group could participate in a reflective practice.

In addition to the general challenges mentioned above, we also encounter challenges more common to CORP. The earliest and most consistent challenge has been enrollment and attendance, with groups running with 5–7 participants on average. The specific challenges of smaller groups are having enough participants for racial affinity spaces and enough diversity of participants so no one feels like an outsider (e.g., all but one member being from the same school district). When the group is small and familiar, it can also lead members to be cautious or concerned about discussing particular issues while still maintaining confidentiality.

Another major pedagogical challenge has been defining the purpose and the processes of the space so that we foster a sense of agency within participants rather than an expectation of being given "solutions" or "answers" to the race-related challenges in their lives. One way this shows up is by participants occasionally responding to a prompt by sharing extensive details about a situation in their life or asking "what do I do?" questions in response to a reflective activity. Our response to this has been to create clear times for "consultation" or dedicated interactive feedback that participants can sign up for. During consultations, we ask participants to come prepared with questions for the group on what they would like feedback on so that we can better focus the conversation. As facilitators, we try to use mindful listening and facilitator listening to support the participants in finding their own "answers." We have also begun emphasizing the importance of allies, co-conspirators (Love, 2019), and collaborators in their real-world lives; in other words, encouraging participants to foster community and explore their important questions more directly with the people in their day-to-day lives.

And finally, we want to honor and highlight the fact that CORP was born during the COVID-19 pandemic and that participants were managing all of the competing needs that multiple pandemics present. We found that nearly everyone was dedicated to regular attendance and engaged participation; however, Zoom fatigue, burnout, uncertainty, and the like were present in the work as well. To address this, we tried to keep the space open and flexible while maintaining the work of racial justice. For example, one of our sessions met on the first day of school for a district that was returning to in-person attendance for the first time since COVID-19 started. We were impressed with the participants' dedication to CORP, but we also chose to pivot our plans for that session to spend some time on self-care.

CRITICAL ELEMENTS OF PROMISE

One of the advantages of CORP is that every single participant has already taken HTAR and therefore has a foundation for dialogues about race and schooling. Regardless of when they took HTAR, participants come to CORP with a shared language and an epistemic trust that enables quicker development of relationships and community. One way that we transfer skills from HTAR to CORP is to maintain the important rituals of opening with a grounding exercise and doing a land acknowledgment as well as a Black Lives Matter (BLM) acknowledgment. However, in CORP, participants may choose to go beyond witnessing acknowledgements as modeled by the facilitators and to present or practice these activities themselves. For some, it may be an exciting opportunity to share a well-known resource or elevate a familiar project; for others, it may be the first time they are putting these tools into practice. Regardless, it is a rich opportunity for participants to build confidence using tools from HTAR while also learning from each other.

As facilitators of both HTAR and CORP, one of the greatest rewards is building relationships with participants over time and witnessing the progression of their journeys. Take, for example, a public-school teacher who shared their first racial autobiography with us in HTAR, then returned to CORP to seek support from others as they gradually defined their action space for racial justice within their own school. This evolution is a testament to the multiple and varied ways that RISE for Racial Justice supports participants across many stages of the journey in racial justice.

As listed above, one of the tensions we hold as a community is the desire to take meaningful action while being mindful of action bias. Although we encourage participants to stay mindful about institutional racism, we also want to maintain awareness of the potential desire to find "quick fixes" or to avoid the discomfort of how endemic and internalized racism is. Critical moments of growth related to this tension are when participants shift away from attempts to take direct action on a person or system and shift their focus to include their own personal actions, beliefs, and biases. For example, we regularly witness participants move from frustration and powerlessness about a particular situation or system and toward a deeper awareness about their role and agency within that "problem."

Another benefit of CORP and its flexible design is our ability as facilitators to take the time to reflect on each session, to seek input from each other, and to return to a point in another class for further dialogue. For example, after one affinity space activity, we both felt disappointed by the conversations in our respective groups; Brett felt frustrated by her inability in the white affinity space to keep the focus on race and to move the group through guilt and toward a more objective reflection about microaggressions, and Masumi felt frustrated by their late recognition that the needs of the conversation were different from the goal of the activity. At our next facilitator meeting, we consulted with each other about how to have more effective affinity spaces. From there, we adapted our plan to return to the same affinity groups in a way that helped the groups evolve and progress, before moving to new topics.

Finally, the partnership between the facilitators and the parallel process of our own reflective practice and planning for action within CORP have been immensely valuable learning experiences. Over time, in our planning meetings, we have built our own brave space as co-facilitators in which we share personal experiences, support each other's action outside of CORP, and hold each other accountable. By observing and supporting each other in practice, we grow in our facilitation skills as well as in our own racial literacies. As a result, our working relationship allows us to model to participants the same tools and growth we hope to foster in CORP participants.

LESSONS LEARNED AND RECOMMENDED ADJUSTMENTS TO CORP

As we write this chapter during the 2021–2022 academic year, we are currently on our third version of CORP. The most significant change for the whole program was our increased commitment to the reflection component of the Community of *Reflective* Practice. In order to support the community in their own processes of reflection, we made the following two adaptations.

Shifting Course Material

Our first version of CORP focused strongly on reviewing material from HTAR and had more of a teacher-centered didactic approach. We even chose tools, activities, and readings for each of the six sessions that directly aligned with the six sessions of HTAR. One initial aspect that we built in was an arc of *action research* that had explicit processes and the following steps (Ferrance, 2000):

1. Identification of a problem area
2. Collection and organization of data
3. Interpretation of data
4. Action based on data
5. Reflection

In addition to reviewing HTAR content, we sequenced each class on a particular step of action research. As a formal reading and point of reference, we used the "Action Research" booklet from Brown University (Ferrance, 2000) for stages of our work.

While it was informative to introduce an action research project, we also noticed that the process of teaching about action research emphasized the teaching over collaborating with participants. Additionally, the time-based aspect of the course did not reflect the realistic timeline one would need to implement an action research topic in a meaningful way. With time and our own reflection, we found it more useful to be guided by the principles of action research (e.g., inquiry, collaboration, evaluation) rather than it being a major focus or structure of CORP.

In the place of action research, we pivoted toward using tools that focused more explicitly on one's lived experiences and circumstances. Of those tools, we used Bobbie Harro's (2000) cycles of socialization and liberation and Deepa Iyer's (2020) ecosystem map. Harro's cycles provide a framework to understand our socialized context and how we are incentivized to not challenge the status quo; it further points us toward an alternative cycle based around principles of community and connection to take action. Through looking at the Harro cycles, participants are able to identify core moments and choice points in their past and in their future where they can take action for racial justice. Iyer's ecosystems map provides participants multiple points of entry into social justice work. Her mapping tool makes the point that there is not one right way to show up, but that everyone has unique talents and gifts that, when combined with others, are necessary for a healthy and flourishing social justice movement.

Adjusting Homework

When we first started CORP, we assigned a significant amount of homework. We asked them to reread readings from HTAR in addition to assigning them new readings and assignments. Each participant was instructed to have their own action research project based on racial justice in their school. In between sessions, their homework included submitting their research questions and methods of inquiry. We hoped that the homework would help them think through their project with feedback, and in each session they reported back on their progress.

We discovered that reassigning readings from HTAR was an incredibly impactful experience. Participants expressed that on second reading, materials from HTAR came alive in a new way. Further, they appreciated the opportunity to process the readings in a small group to understand them deeper.

While the homework aspect of CORP had many benefits, we ultimately felt that the homework load was asking a lot of participants, especially in the context of the competing participant needs we mentioned earlier. We wanted to make CORP feel more like a community where people could come to talk through their work, more than a continued academic experience. With that in mind, we rebranded future CORP versions as being a homework-free community.

CONCLUSION

Perhaps the most defining aspect of CORP is its reflective element, which was representative both in the participants' work as well as our parallel process as facilitators. As facilitators, we constantly learned from our participants, and, with their feedback, co-created a course that was ever evolving. We watched CORP adapt as our collective dreams and aspirations for it also adapted. Through the process of planning and teaching the latest iteration of CORP, we were also writing this chapter together. It manifested as weekly meetings where we both reflected on and planned our existing class *and* got to have larger-picture conversations about the goals of our work and how we wanted to frame it. This chapter, rather than being a picture of a pristine program, also played an important role in the shaping of CORP. We look forward to the future versions of CORP, in whatever shape they take, and are grateful for this powerful opportunity to capture our process in writing.

REFERENCES

Arao, B., & Clemens, K. (2013). From safe spaces to brave spaces. In L. M. Landreman (Ed.), *The art of effective facilitation: Reflections from social justice educators* (pp. 135–150). Stylus Publishing.

Dewey, J. (1966). *Democracy and education: An introduction to the philosophy of education.* The Free Press.

Ferrance, E. (2000). *Themes in education: Action research.* Providence. Northeast and Islands Regional Educational Laboratory.

Finlay, L. (2008). Reflecting on 'reflective practice'. *Practice-based Professional Learning Paper 52.* The Open University.

Harro, B. (2000). The cycle of socialization. In M. Adams, W. Blumenfeld, R. Castaneda, H. Hackman, M. Peters, & X. Zúñiga (Eds.), *Readings for diversity and social justice* (pp. 16–21). Routledge.

Heffron, M. C., & Murch, T. (2010). *Reflective supervision and leadership for infant and early childhood programs*. Zero to Three.

Iyer, D. (2020). *Mapping our roles in social change ecosystems*. Accessed on January 1, 2022, from http://deepaiyer.com/the-map-social-change-ecosystem.

Love, B. (2019). *We want to do more than survive: Abolitionist teaching and the pursuit of educational freedom*. Beacon Press.

Magee, R. (2019). *The inner work of racial justice: Healing ourselves and transforming our communities through mindfulness*. TarcherPerigee.

Schön, D. A. (1983). *The reflective practitioner: How professionals think in action*. Basic Books.

CHAPTER 6

The Importance of Intergroup-Dialogue Pedagogy for Antiracist K–12 Classrooms

A Focus on Teaching Educators Facilitation Skills

Meredith Madden

In summer 2021, RISE for Racial Justice created a new space for K–12 educators. The space was for and about intergroup dialogue. It was not solely a space for having dialogues, though that organically happened. It was an intentional space for educators to gain dialogic pedagogical skills for their classrooms. These were largely K–12 classroom spaces, but we recognize that educational spaces transcend classroom borders and that dialogue is important in co-curricular spaces as well. The decision to create a course on dialogue stemmed from a discussion among the directors about what the next level of literacy training should be for teachers who had completed How to Talk About Race (HTAR), the first antiracism course. In addition to Race Theory and A Community of Reflective Practice, we added another intermediate course for K–12 teachers—one on intergroup dialogue.

Educational research on intergroup dialogue (IGD) (Gurin et al., 2013; Zuniga et al., 2014) shows that IGD pedagogy in classrooms has positive impacts on students' academic and socioemotional learning. The research indicates a direct correlation between IGD practices and reduced stereotypes, prejudices, and biases. The empirical evidence on this specific model of critical dialogue informed the decision to include this as a model for dialogic antiracist training. Thus, Intergroup Dialogue Training for Teachers was created. This course taught educators the four stages of the IGD model, IGD pedagogical practices across the four stages, as well as provided direct practice in using IGD pedagogy and the opportunity to workshop visions for application in each participants' educational space.

FROM WHERE I ENTER

I enter the space of this chapter having designed and co-facilitated the Intergroup Dialogue Training for Teachers course. In writing about this particular journey for me, it is my hope that what is shared here supports educators journeying toward spaces of teaching about race, racism, and antiracism through critical dialogic facilitation. My own genealogy of IGD facilitator preparation is important to share because, as educators, we arrive at moments of invitation to dialogue in unique ways. Reflecting on and sharing my own facilitator preparation positions the reader to bear witness to the process and intention behind IGD facilitation, which reflects the very process- and intention-based foundation from which IGD grows.

As I introduced myself at the beginning of this book, I am a former public-school teacher. This location has informed so much of the work I now do. Before entering graduate school in the Cultural Foundations of Education program at Syracuse University, I taught middle school special education. I began my journey in the Bronx, NY, and ended my journey in Central New York; I ended my profession of teaching *in* public schools, but I knew I wanted to continue to teach *for* public schools. I knew that I wanted to remain committed to disrupting educational inequities, but I was not sure what the path would look like for me to get there. I was reminded by the words shared between Horton and Freire (1990) in dialogue about education and social change and the Highlander Folk School, now identified as the Highlander Research and Education Center, that indeed "We make the road by walking." So I walked. And I arrived at the doorstep of intergroup dialogue.

Through my graduate coursework, I learned from Gretchen Lopez, director of Intergroup Dialogue at Syracuse University, about the theory and praxis of the University of Michigan–founded intergroup dialogue model. I was invited to put the theory into practice by being trained at Syracuse as an IGD facilitator and then designing and facilitating the first offering of an intergroup dialogue on socioeconomic inequality and education. I was able to do a deep-dive research project on social class dialogues that affect undergraduate student experiences. What the research named about the positive impacts that IGD had on reducing stereotypes, prejudices, and bias was something I was bearing witness to as a facilitator in my undergraduate classrooms. As I moved to teach as a full-time faculty member on other college campuses, I brought with me my IGD pedagogical practices. These other campuses had not established IGD programs, but that did not mean I couldn't integrate the pedagogical practices into my courses. As I did this, I often reflected back to my time as a public-school teacher. It would have meant a great deal for me and my students if I had had access to IGD pedagogy as a K–12 educator. Moving forward in ways where my actions could match my commitments meant creating spaces for other K–12 educators to access this pedagogical model. As part of my own local community education outreach efforts from 2016 to the present, I have been helping develop career teachers' and pre-service teachers' pedagogy through the IGD model. Building this work into RISE for Racial Justice's national antiracism training is another step on my journey of walking the walk of my antiracist educational commitments.

AN INTERGROUP DIALOGUE TRAINING COURSE FOR TEACHERS

For 6 weeks during the summer of 2021, educators from across the United States joined together remotely in a community to gain pedagogical content knowledge on intergroup dialogue. Though we were forced to offer the course remotely due to COVID-19, this platform allowed the wide range of geographical participation from coast to coast. Some of the teachers knew at least one other person from their home district or had previously learned or taught with one another. We had teachers who taught levels ranging from early childhood to high school and a range of experience in the field from early career educators to veteran teachers. What the teachers in this course had in common was a commitment to building antiracist classrooms and an interest in learning how to use tools from intergroup dialogue to do so. And, of course, they had all taken the introductory course, How to Talk About Race (HTAR).

As noted in the introduction, the IGD model is organized into four stages, as follows:

Stage 1. Group Beginnings: Forming and Building Relationships
Stage 2. Identity, Social Relations, and Conflict
Stage 3. Power, Equity, Fairness, and Inclusion

Stage 4. Alliances, Coalitions, and Empowerment (Gurin et al., 2013)

Intergroup dialogue operates from a place of guiding principles. These include integrating person and structure, exploring commonalities and differences, and linking reflection and action in order to gain knowledge and awareness, as well as the skills necessary to be an active participatory member of society. The RISE for Racial Justice IGD training course was intentional about integrating these principles in praxis. It was critical that what was being taught to the teachers was also being experienced by the teachers.

In the training, teachers were immersed into an IGD experience where they would be able to think and feel their way through IGD pedagogical practices and reflect on how they could use dialogue in their classrooms. To begin, teachers were invited to form a community. This was not going to be a webinar setting nor a "sage on the stage" setting. The IGD training course was about bringing teachers to the center and creating links across experience.

Stage 1. Group Beginnings: Forming and Building Relationships

Beginning with Stage 1, facilitation focused on forming and building community and relationships among the class and modeling the pedagogical practices for doing this work in the teachers' classrooms. During participant introductions, we asked teachers to name their hopes and fears for dialogues about race in the classroom. The introductory sessions called for the use of mindful listening and a commitment to supporting the learning of others in the course. Unlike in HTAR where participants are given a set of norms to follow as a community (see Chapter 3), in this course teachers collaboratively engaged in building community guidelines. These guidelines were a living and breathing set of norms that teachers were invited to visit, revisit, and revise as needed to meet the changing needs and desires of the group. As in HTAR, teachers were encouraged and supported to work always from a stretch zone (the place that pushes them to grow most significantly). These introductory moments in the first sessions were followed by a presentation that answered their question: Just what *is* intergroup dialogue? The intentional framing and engaging of the introductory activities created space for the teachers to experience what they would perhaps ask their own students to experience and, in doing so, shifted their locations from teachers learning about pedagogical content knowledge in the training course to teachers *experiencing* the pedagogical content knowledge in the training course.

The facilitation of Stage 1 required a continued commitment to building teachers' racial literacy and adding an IGD literacy in specific ways. Their background from HTAR positioned them to reflect, revisit, and continue to grow their understanding of key terms and language. This literacy included language on personal and social identity; socialization; and power, privilege, and oppression. It also included a nuanced dialogue on the term "dialogue" itself. Intergroup dialogue, we remind people, is not debate. It is working from a place of informed knowing, awareness-raising, and deep listening. That is a place that requires a literacy that HTAR offered, nurtured, and supported.

Stage 2. Identity, Social Relations, and Conflict

As the course developed, the teachers were guided through Stage 2. Working through each stage, teachers gained pedagogical content knowledge about each stage and had opportunities to engage with pedagogical methods and again, reflect and dialogue on applications for these pedagogical methods in their classroom space. Two critical pedagogical activities from this stage of the course included a social identity activity called the social identity wheel (similar to the power flower described in Chapter 3) and an activity on identity, culture, and community called the "culture chest."

The culture chest is an act of storytelling. Participants "reflect on and speak about the significance of a range of social identities that affect their lives, including the ones that are the foci of the dialogue. Because the culture chest emphasizes storytelling and speaking and listening, this activity often deepens the level of sharing and relationship building in the group" (Zúñiga et al., 2007, p. 94). This activity is very important for teachers to participate in before they bring it to their classrooms. One cannot anticipate the level of deep thinking and feeling that this activity induces until it is experienced. For teachers, the identity of "teacher" might feel enough to connect them to other teachers in a training. However, this activity peels back and unpacks the lived experiences of each person behind the identity "teacher," and in doing so, creates powerful spaces to truly see one another. This seeing is necessary for community spaces that hold vulnerability, empathy, and care at the center. This seeing is also a good perspective for teachers to have so that if they bring this into their classrooms they can anticipate how their students might experience the sharing, listening, and community building.

Stage 3. Power, Equity, Fairness, and Inclusion

Upon completion of the second stage, the course moved teachers to Stage 3. This stage is often called "Hot Topics" in IGD programs because students bring in articles to share and facilitate dialogues that are usually "hot" or divided by perspective. For the training course, participants leave with a full understanding of the process of the third stage. Given that time is somewhat limited, this course organizes around preselected texts that participants engage with before participating in a "hot topic" dialogic activity. The text selections are informed by teachers' interests based on what they are experiencing on the front lines of education every day as classroom teachers.

Another critical moment of IGD pedagogy training occurred in Stage 3 with an activity called the "gallery walk." As with earlier described pedagogical activities, the gallery walk activity can be found in a broad range of critical pedagogical classroom and organizational spaces. It is intentionally used in IGD spaces because of its usefulness in bringing multiple, diverse perspectives into the learning space and providing a springboard for sustained critical dialogue that can promote perspective taking. Within the course, the gallery walk was initially a challenge because of the online setting. What in the classroom might take the shape of students' representations (written or artistic, displayed on poster boards) to an assigned reading, viewing or listening would need to take a different shape in the online classroom space. Instead, the teachers created an online gallery by responding to text on racism and education through virtual visual and oral presentation. Through a collaborative online document, teachers' names were displayed and, one by one, they built a gallery by voicing their statements, statistics, quotes, and questions. The class read and responded to the online gallery and used a "popcorn" participation approach, sharing their own thoughts and then inviting in someone else to share. A line was drawn to electronically connect the names of each participant on the online document so that the teachers could visualize the building of dialogue across the activity.

Stage 4. Alliances, Coalitions, and Empowerment

This training course came to a soft close with Stage 4. It is a soft close because we know that the work is never done. Earlier in Stage 2 of the course, teachers engaged with Harro's (2000) work on the cycle of oppression. At Stage 4, the teachers move their work to engaging

Harro's (2000) cycle of liberation. What the course prepared teachers for was to know and understand the cycle of oppression early on and then arrive at Stage 4 thinking and engaging with the concept of liberation. In this concluding part of the training course, teachers actively engage the ways that they can be agents of social change as active participants, allies, and co-conspirators in the cycle of liberation. Our hope is that teachers who complete this course have new tools to create spaces of racial justice in their classrooms and the legacy of dialogue in action will carry forward to make transformative possibilities in education.

REFERENCES

Gurin, P., Nagda, B. (R.) A., & Zúñiga, X. (2013). *Dialogue across difference: Practice, theory, and research on intergroup dialogue.* Russell Sage Foundation.

Harro, B. (2000). The cycle of socialization. In M. Adams, W. Blumenfeld, R. Castaneda, H. Hackman, M. Peters, & X. Zúñiga (Eds.), *Readings for diversity and social justice* (pp. 16–21). Routledge.

Horton, M., & Freire, P. (1990). *We make the road by walking: Conversations on education and social change* (Eds. B. Bell, J. Gaventa, & J. Peters). Temple University Press.

Zúñiga, X., Lopez, G. E., & Ford, K. A. (2014). *Intergroup dialogue: Engaging difference, social identities, and social justice.* Routledge.

Zúñiga, X., Nagda, B. A., Chesler, M., & Cytron-Walker, A. (2007). *Intergroup dialogue in higher education: Meaningful learning about social justice.* ASHE Higher Education Report.

CHAPTER 7

Let's Talk About Race

An Antiracism Course for Youth

Meredith Madden

The summer of 2020 was a summer of racial reckoning when people were called to reckon with race and the work they do or do not do to disrupt racism from where they stand. This is not to say that everyone answered (or even heard) the call. It is to say that many did hear it and worked to answer it. It is important to understand the multiple, diverse responses to the racial reckoning of the summer of 2020. It is critical to consider how people responded to the call if we are to understand the processes of racial reckoning. This understanding is imperative for those working to end systemic racism. What did folks do with what they had and from where they were located in the summer of 2020? After all, racial reckoning is not a one-stop journey. So just how did people respond? And what was the role of community educators in guiding folks through that response?

For the past decade I have been located on Haudenosaunee land in a small rural/suburban Central New York town just shy of 2,000 residents. Heading west out of town will lead you to a middle-class suburban area that opens the way to consumer squares and, eventually, 20 miles later, to a small city. Heading east of town you enter the expansive countryside of rural New York State with its agriculture industry.

Residents share land with a small private liberal arts college that perches atop "the hill." It is a predominantly white college that looks down over a predominately white town situated within a predominantly white pocket of New York State. This is politically a red area and appears to be increasingly so, which reflects growing trends in rural voters identifying with the Republican party. With this identification comes more conservative views on social issues. For example, a 2020 public opinion survey reported by Dina Smeltz with *The Chicago Council on Global Affairs* reveals that only 23% of Republicans think racial inequality is a "critical threat to the country"—a finding in stark contrast to the 73% of Democrats who consider racial inequality to be a "critical threat to the country" (Smeltz, 2020).

RESPONDING TO THE CALL FOR RACIAL JUSTICE

In summer 2020, the summer of racial reckoning, when during a pandemic folks were quite literally forced to stay where they were and see the world in front of them, one must ask what that meant for *how* people experienced the call for racial justice and the vehicle they took to move forward on their journey in the movement for racial justice.

Responding to the call for racial reckoning, one parent in Central New York contacted me to inquire about the possibility of my leading a course on race, racism, and antiracism for community youth. Inquiring about my community education course was one parent's answer to the call for racial reckoning. I agreed to teach the course and got to work organizing a curriculum for young people while the parent connected with her children's friends to look for other interested youth to join the course. I created a flyer to publicize the summer course, which I shared largely on social media so that any youth in the community could apply. The course did not have a set fee, and I offered the course through a donation-based payment model because I didn't want money to be a barrier to any young person's participation.

Before reflecting on the course, it is critical that I name my positionality and how I enter this space of community education on race. I am a white, able-bodied woman who has lived largely in the northeastern United States. I have had a fluid social-class identity that has moved between working class and middle class. I have had a fluid faith identity fluctuating between Catholicism and noninstitutional spirituality. I am also the parent of a teenager. Parenting a teenager in the summer of 2020 gave me a lens to view the ways youth were desperate for spaces of connection to communicate about what was happening around them in the world. Since spaces for critical analytical conversations can be few and far between in formal educational spaces, I have seen how social media creates a space for critical conversations on societal topics, including and especially on race and racism.

As a parent I know the feeling of wanting to give opportunities to your children to critically think on social issues and give them space to imagine how they may participate in society as agents of social change. As an activist-scholar-mother, my own social location positioned me to understand how critical it is that youth have access to a facilitated space on race and racism largely because I understand that a lack of racial literacy is a barrier to people feeling prepared for and engaging in these crucial dialogues. I had been leading race, racism, and antiracism community education courses for teachers for over a year, and I was eager to be of service to young folks for their own personal development, for the good of the community and society at large. I recognized that in the predominately white, right-wing locale of Central New York, many folks felt stuck and unsure of how to move forward toward antiracism. How do we unglue our white minds from the pavement of white supremacy that we have been born and raised on? The racial reckoning of the summer of 2020 was a call for me to continue to demonstrate my racial justice activism in public educational spaces. I would protest racism in society by doing what I have been encouraged by my mentors to do and doing what I have advised my mentees to do: Start where you are. And so, I would protest racism in schools by teaching about racism and antiracism to teen-aged students. I would do my part, inspired by critical pedagogue Freire (1985), to create a space for youth to read their world so that they could be writers of the world, with the hope that they would write toward racial equity and justice.

Protest means to move objection or disapproval into action. The race class for youth was a class that embodied the term "protest." The course in and of itself was a statement of disapproval, disagreement, complaint, and objection to racism in the United States. Youth learning in this course represented the verb "protest" because through learning about race, racism, and antiracism, youth could use the tool of their developed racial literacy to express their objection and then stand in full resistance and opposition to the reality of a racist world. They could proclaim a vision for another way, a *just* way, coupled with actionable strategies for learning against racism in their formalized public-school spaces.

DEVELOPING AND TEACHING A COURSE FOR YOUTH

Having led community education courses for local educators for over a year and teaching social justice education in education departments in higher education for a decade, I entered my work knowing the general goals for the course I would design for youth. Let's Talk About Race for Youth was developed as a 4-week course designed in response to a need for youth (grades 9–12) to raise their awareness on race, racism, antiracism, and racial justice. This course would aim to give students key language and knowledge on select race topics as well as antiracist skills and strategies. Students would be guided by two overarching questions—*What stories have you been told,* and *what stories will you tell?*—and do so using a counterstory framework inspired by the work of Bell (2010). The course would use minilectures, dialogic pedagogy, and an action component to examine race and racism and work to build racially just spaces in the students' communities.

A critical component of the class would be the inclusion of a workshop on brainstorming and proposing a racial justice action project. The action project was inspired by the IGD education model that is anchored in critical pedagogy and concludes the curriculum with an action project to move what former Syracuse University chancellor Nancy Cantor named *scholarship in action*. This type of project empowers students to move theory to practice and in the process teaches them agency over their own ideas, commitments, and work. Students in Let's Talk About Race for Youth would be taken through the various pieces of a racial justice action project proposal and given space to create their own antiracist action project. The overarching goals were for students to leave the course with increased content knowledge and racial literacy, increased racial identity awareness, and a concrete proposal for an antiracist project that could be used in their home educational setting.

Rationale for Course Design

The course was designed with intention based on my experiences teaching social justice in two spaces. The first space was at Syracuse University, where I facilitated an IGD course on socioeconomic inequality in education over 4 years. From that experience I learned that students of all ages who gain a social justice literacy, experience learning activities that illuminate their own socialization processes, and engage in a social action project have positive outcomes including consciousness raising, increased identity awareness, and calls and engaged responses to social action (Madden, 2015).

Having also developed and taught the course Education, Teaching and Social Change at Hamilton College, I also drew on IGD pedagogical methods coupled with Bell's (2010) *Storytelling for Social Justice*. I observed the positive impact on students' learning to identify stock stories and locate and name the counterstories when examining lived experiences anchored in social identities such as race. Across the years of my teaching this course, I heard from undergraduates how they would have benefited from having had access to this type of pedagogy and learning earlier in their educational experiences. Many undergraduates felt opportunities for social change had been missed by not having discussions on racial and social injustices during their earlier youth in middle and high school settings. With this knowledge, I chose to apply the framework with an "earlier on" age group through a college-community-partnership program I direct called CNY Writes: Centering Narratives of Youth. The numerous CNY Writes workshops over the past 4 years affirmed that youth were eager for spaces of their own to process their lived experiences. In fact, a few CNY Writes workshops had drawn youth from Central New York who were especially anxious to gain language and strategies to identify what they were experiencing around social identity and lived experience. Fast forward to the summer of 2020 and these reflections provided me with a rationale for not only why the youth course on race, racism, and antiracism was needed but also how, if delivered through a social justice framework, it could truly result in positive learning outcomes for new students. As I expressed in Chapter 6, I knew that my earlier work would make the road on which I was called to walk, and now that road had led me in August 2020 to a Zoom room filled with eight white youth from rural/suburban Central New York.

Logistics of the Course

The course met four times across 4 weeks and used an online virtual classroom to organize and disseminate materials. After each class, I sent a post-class memo to each participant. Additionally, given the youth were under the age of 18 and were taking the course from home, I made an intentional decision to also email a post-class memo to those parenting them following each class. When youth learn about these topics during in-person educational settings—for example, at the colleges where I have taught—there are resources available for emotional support and counseling should any student need them. I wanted to make sure parents understood what their children were learning about so that they could be a process partner for their child and offer them emotional support as they navigated new learning.

Class 1. The first class centered largely on building community and introducing key terms. Some of the participants were familiar with one another already, but across the whole group, everyone was new to at least two other participants. For those who knew one another prior to the course, there were varied levels of acquaintance. This made establishing a community in the online space critical. To begin, all participants identified something they hoped to get out of this experience, something they felt unsure about, and something that they felt very sure about.

The group also began class by building a set of community guidelines. There was a focus on the importance of bravery in this shared space. The first class was anchored largely to key terms and language. It was important to me that the participants knew they had space to ask many questions about language and clarify any terms that they suspected were offensive or outdated. This moment required vulnerability to identify terms, and a benefit of an online space is the use of the chat feature that keeps questions directly between the participant and the facilitator. In this way, participants could communicate directly with me and ask about a specific term. I could then raise the term and discuss it with the whole group without identifying the participant by name. There was a significant amount of communication and learning around key terms that I doubt would have happened without the private online chat option.

During Class 1, participants also learned about racism in its many forms. I knew from my work with adults over the past year that systemic racism is a specific type of racism that many white folks have grown up never having heard about, let alone knowing about or understanding. Teaching this class meant meeting the responsibility of defining this term and illuminating the ways the system works to reproduce and sustain legacies of oppression, including racism, by using a point of analysis they all could grasp: school. The participants were familiar with the term "systemic racism" through online media during the summer of 2020. They had heard the term, and had glimpses of understanding what it meant, but wanted to understand it more fully. Grasping this term was necessary because all subsequent classes would involve a racial-equity analysis anchored to systems.

Finally, and crucially, the participants learned about the process of socialization. A central point of this course is that we cannot begin to examine someone else's lived experience unless we have done the work to first unpack and understand our own. For our class, there would be no examining the lived experiences of BIPOC until the youth had discussed whiteness and white supremacy and understood what it meant to hold a white racial identity as white people. The youth reflected on their own social identities and had dialogue on the ways their white racial identity located them in their schools and the education system at large and what holding this identity meant for how they experienced learning and school. A useful activity was asking the participants to first examine the way their racial identity impacted their educational experiences. Then they were asked to consider their racial identity at the intersection of another social identity (such as gender, faith, class) and examine the ways the intersecting identities impacted their educational experiences. This was the first introduction to the term "intersectionality," and participants were able to apply intersectionality to their own experiences. The close of Class 1 set up a strong transition to Classes 2 and 3, which addressed topics of power, privilege, and oppression.

Classes 2 and 3. In the next two classes the participants added to their racial literacy by gaining knowledge about white privilege, racial microaggressions, and implicit bias. Building on their work in Class 1, where they examined their own intersectional identities in context of power, privilege, and oppression, students watched and dialogued on a video of a privilege walk (As/Is, 2015). A privilege walk is an awareness-raising activity that invites everyone to stand next to one another in a straight line. A facilitator asks questions anchored to lived experience that illuminate advantages and disadvantages. Participants move either forward or backward depending on their response. Responses that reveal a person's experience anchored to privilege and advantage are met with people stepping forward. Responses that reveal a person's experience anchored to oppression and disadvantage are met with people stepping backward. By the end of the video the participants are no longer side by side but standing in different places that represent clear distinctions of privilege and oppression across social identity groups. People in the video reflect on the experience of the activity and the ways awareness was raised about systems of oppression. Participants in the course reflect on their own awareness raising as a result of engaging with the privilege walk video.

Privilege walk activities are often rooted in scholarship on privilege such as Peggy McIntosh's "The Invisible Knapsack" (1990). Participants turned to discussion of McIntosh's article after reading it as a homework assignment. This article was accessible for all the participants and raised awareness on white privilege through concrete examples that were applicable to the students' lives. To extend this, I incorporated a learning activity where all students constructed their own knapsacks and identified what was in their invisible knapsacks while being sure to include examples that pertained to their educational experiences. Classes 2 and 3 required an in-depth examination of one's own socialization, and this led to a moment of learning about racial microaggressions and implicit bias. These conversations are often not part of the socialization of young white people, and that very point was discussed during the class:

- What does it mean to avoid and remove discussion of race, power, and privilege?
- What is the relationship between that avoidance and removal and oppression?
- How does that ignorance lead to racial microaggressions and implicit bias?

These class sessions were also the central places that participants were charged with identifying the single stories of their lived experiences. To begin, participants viewed Chimamanda Ngozi Adichie's 2009 TED talk, "The Danger of a Single Story" (Adichie, 2009), where they heard how showing people, places, and things as one thing over and over again can reduce people, places, and things to one idea, a single story. To create dignity and justice means to identify single stories and then disrupt them. Participants discussed where they saw single stories revealed in their educational settings from individual to interpersonal experiences, or entrenched systemically in many of the books they read or the Eurocentric lessons they were taught.

Bell (2010) is one of many social justice educators who urges the telling of counterstories and resistance stories to combat single stories. The participants engaged with in-depth dialogue on stock stories and concealed stories, specifically in education. To write counterstories to their educational experiences, this group transitioned to the fourth and final class, where they created action plan proposals.

Class 4. We began the last class with a dialogue on solidarity. This was a learning moment about what it means to be in an activist community with others with shared commitments to something like racial equity and justice. It was important for the young people to realize that, during a pandemic and a time of increased isolation, there are others with the same yearnings and commitments to racial equity and justice in their town.

This final class gave me the opportunity to share with students a learning activity that I often use in my college classrooms, where experiential learning is central to the curriculum. The format was a workshop that moved the ideas that had been percolating for the students into a vision for action and transformation in their home schools. This learning activity was adapted from the curriculum I used when teaching an IGD course at Syracuse University.

The youth came to the last class with an idea for an actionable project they wanted to create and implement in the 2020–2021 school year. During the workshop, I took the youth through all of the pieces of an action plan proposal, and they took time to write their own proposals. To do this, they crafted a statement of the problem, identified the need, and crafted their plan goals and objectives. Next, they developed their step-by-step action plan, as well as developed a list of resources from which they could draw to develop, implement, and assess their projects. They also developed a list of what challenges they might face and thought in advance of who might be allies to help them navigate those challenges in their schools and communities. Some worked independently and others worked in small groups. All had the opportunity to share their proposal with the whole group and get feedback. There was discussion about meeting up halfway through the year to do a check-in and provide additional support as needed to one another. In this final meeting, the class intentionally created space for reflection, check-ins, and once again naming our action-oriented intention for moving this work into the public.

As Let's Talk About Race for Youth came to an end, there was a great deal of discussion about how everyone felt sitting with their new information and their action plan. In a single summer month, these young folks had developed so much awareness. There was also a great deal of discussion about hope. Was there still hopelessness felt as it had been felt by them when entering the class? There was. This was no different than most of the experiences I have had teaching—people often feel so hopeless around issues of inequity and assaults on justice and human rights, especially when they realize the role of systems in inequity and injustice. However, there is a shift in the hopelessness, a shift toward reaffirming commitments and taking steps forward in action. And that shift gives all of us hope.

We closed our last class together by reading the words of U.S. Representative Alexandria Ocasio-Cortez (2019): "You can't wait for hope. You have to BE hope." We are all hope. We can all be hope. As I logged off my computer that evening, I knew a bit more of what I had always believed to be true on the journey toward racial equity and justice: young people are the hope of the world.

CRITICAL MOMENT OF CHALLENGE: SUSTAINING SOLIDARITY

In reflecting back on the month of classes, one thing I was very aware of was that most of the youth attended the same small school district. There was no clear sense that they were friends, though it was clear that there were a few pairs of close contacts and that the students who attended the same school district knew of one another. Across the month, it appeared that the invisible borders that separated peers such as grade level and town lines disappeared as the students began to focus on what brought them to this virtual space: their commitment to racial equity and justice. As the facilitator, a critical moment of challenge for me was realizing that this course was just a moment in time and knowing that it was not long enough to perhaps build solidarity in ways that would be sustainable. I know that solidarity is powerful, and I was grateful the youth experienced it, even for a month's time, so that they could recognize it and nurture it in their future work. Still, I was faced with the real challenge of knowing that what had been created across the four weeks could easily slip away. I was challenged and am still challenged to think about how I can do this work with youth in ways that make this not a fleeting, immersive, and performative experience, but instead sustainable and actionable. It will therefore be important for me to reconvene this group of students to have a check-in and give them space to share the progress of their action projects. Given the pandemic, I know that some of their action plans may have been disrupted or put on hold until in-person schooling resumes. The challenge then is also how to be or remain actionable during a pandemic and in virtual spaces.

CRITICAL MOMENTS OF PROMISE

The Invitation

I found it particularly promising that at the outset of this journey a parent reached out to me. There are invitations to make an impact in the lives of others that come in many forms. This particular invitation arrived in the form of a message on social media. It was an invitation wrapped up in a brief inquiry about whether or not I would ever teach my community education classes for youth. During the summer of 2020, I was also trying to make sense of my own activism and where to pour my energy. I found it particularly brave that this mother contacted me, and I found promise in her invitation. If she was looking for a resource for the young people in her life nestled in a very right-leaning, predominately white, rural/suburban Central New York town, then there were others. I was sure of it. That realization is one of promise.

Giving the Language

One of the most *promising* moments about the Let's Talk About Race for Youth course was that it gave the language to young folks who may otherwise not have received it for another 3 to 4 years or so if by chance they were to take a college course in the humanities or social sciences or have another similar educational experience. As educators it is our responsibility to teach in a way that builds literacy for students so that they can read the world and read the word as Freire (1985) shared. We also want them to have the agency to write the world. The white youth who took this course on race, racism, and antiracism in a right-wing rural/suburban Central New York town knew they needed the language, and their *parents and caregivers* knew they needed the language.

I also knew they needed the language *now*. In the fight for racial equity and justice there is no privilege of time. The young folks heard the cries for racial justice that summer, and they responded by coming to the class, sharing the complex and painful things they bore witness to in educational and community spaces, and showing up to receive the lessons, the language, and the literacy to prepare them to be agents of change for racial equity and justice. It reminded me so much of what I was told when I facilitated the IGD course at Syracuse University. I listened each week to the young folks' awareness on issues from lack of representation in textbooks and curricula to wondering why it was that not all of their teachers disrupted racist moments of harm. Now they knew what they knew. Their consciousness was raised. They would have an increased literacy to name, examine, and understand their experiences. The promise of the power that lies with that matters now and in the future.

RECOMMENDATIONS AND VISIONS

Partnership

One recommendation for a future version of this course is to have this be a sequenced course. The first course would remain similar to what is currently developed. However, the second course in the sequence would involve a partnership with a local college. As a college educator, I witness undergraduate and graduate students grow in their activism every day. College campuses can be profound sites of activism. This partnership work might involve the high school students' partnering on a shared vision for change in the local community. Collectively with their multiple, diverse knowledges and experience, this group could work in solidarity around racial equity and justice. A second course would also afford the facilitator to have more time working with the students and creating spaces of sustainable solidarity.

Parental, Caregiver, and Mentor Involvement

As I mentioned earlier, I included parents and caregivers in the course by sending them a post-class memo on what their children had learned in class. There was space for students to also identify a mentor in their life to be included, and I recommend that for this course in the future. In the post-class memo, I shared links to everything that we viewed as well as provided copies of the readings. I did this so parents could keep the conversation going with their youth in their home spaces. I did not doubt parent support. However, I do not know what racial literacy the parents had. In some respects that meant trusting that the students would teach their parents when the conversations happened and if they happened at all. What if parents themselves were under-prepared for these conversations and this work? I knew conversations might arise at home that would help reinforce the students' under-standing and learning, but I envision for the future recommending that parents register for our parallel parent course as a way to further support both groups of learners.

Adaption of Course for RISE for Racial Justice

It was clear to me that this course would benefit from having more homes. As my work in the field of antiracist education began to connect to others doing the work, I saw an opportunity to offer an adaption of this course in other spaces too. In conversation with RISE for Racial Justice, the invitation to adapt this course and include it in the Rise curriculum presented itself. In spring 2021, Rise included the course in the curriculum and offered this course for youth. Through online synchronous facilitation, I was able to facilitate the course for high school students on the West coast. The work was engaging and transformative for the youth and myself. For one, the youth course was now being built into another antiracist training structure with RISE for Racial Justice. Second, the youth were able to conceptualize action plans to move antiracist practices into their own educational institutions.

The recommendation for all this work is that it remains actionable and sustainable. It is clear that many youth are unwilling to compromise on whether or not talking about race and developing antiracist practices is important. So many are clear that it is. When high school students who took the course were asked by a school administrator if all the students in the school should take this course, the response was overwhelmingly "Yes!" They even recommended that the course be taken earlier, at the middle school level. If we plant the seeds of hope as action early on in education, then the blooms are more likely to be blooms of dignity, humanity, and justice.

REFERENCES

Adichie, C. N. (2009). The danger of a single story (Video). TED Conferences. Retrieved January 10, 2022, from https://www.ted.com/talks/chimamanda_ngozi_adichie_the_danger_of_a_single_story?utm_campaign=tedspread&utm_medium=referral&utm_source=tedcomshare.

As/Is. (2015, July 4). *What is Privilege?* (Video). YouTube. https://youtu.be/hD5f8GuNuGQ.

Bell, L. A. (2010). *Storytelling for social justice: Connecting narrative and the arts in antiracist teaching.* Routledge.

Freire, P. (1985). Reading the world and reading the word: An interview with Paulo Freire. *Language Arts, 62*(1).

Madden, M. (2015). Social class dialogues and the fostering of class consciousness. *Equity & Excellence in Education, 48*(4), 571–588.

McIntosh, P. (1990). White privilege: Unpacking the invisible knapsack. *Independent School, 49*(2), 31–36.

Ocasio-Cortez, A. [@AOC]. (2019, May 29). *You can't wait for hope. You have to be hope.* [tweet]. Twitter. https://twitter.com/AOC/status/113388552267 2267264?s=20&t=8N3GIzPdyQXNGXgWlMI2XQ.

Smeltz, D. (2020, October 19). Republican views on racial inequality starkly contrast those of Democrats. *The Chicago Council of Global Affairs*. Retrieved January 10, 2022, from https://www.thechicagocouncil .org/research/public-opinion-survey/republican-views-racial-inequality -starkly-contrast-those-democrats.

Building the Arc of White Womanhood

Robin Mallison Alpern

Most of my life, I have navigated between focusing on feminism and antiracism. The middle of three daughters, I was raised in the 1950s–60s in a middle-class white family in northern New York State. My Quaker parents, Carolyn and Glenn Mallison, taught my sisters and me that all people are inherently equal. Racial prejudice (as it was called then) was wrong, and our family was active in work to improve "race relations."

At age 16, I was invited by my mother to her feminist, consciousness-raising group. Feminism became my organizing principle for the next decade. As a child, I had acquired the unspoken belief that a boy was worth two girls. The feminist movement encouraged me to name and push back against sexism. I was particularly focused on issues of rape—though not as a survivor. I researched the topic, published letters to editors, and briefly worked at a local rape crisis hotline. I also became deeply interested in literature on the contributions womxn had made to our culture, contributions largely buried by the patriarchal narrative.

Over the years, internal and external events caused my pendulum to swing from feminism to race issues and back. It didn't seem, at the time, that I could or should be engaged in both movements at once. My socialization suggested I ought to have a priority issue, and these two seemed like separate concerns.

Then in the early 2000s, I attended a Quaker conference where a Black Friend (Quaker) took me aside to recount several instances where she had been discriminated against in our Quaker community. Though I listened sympathetically, I thought to myself she must have exaggerated or misunderstood the incidents she described. But

6 months later, a Black member of another group I belonged to shared similar stories of racial prejudice in that community. I began to understand that this was not an exaggeration or misunderstanding. This was not the fault of Black individuals. Racism existed in these spaces that I held dear, spaces full of good, well-intentioned white people.

Soon after, at another Quaker conference, I attended an antiracist workshop led by an interracial couple, Charley Flint (Black) and Jeff Hitchcock (white). They had founded the Center for the Study of White American Culture (CSWAC) to decenter whiteness and build multiracial antiracist community. I asked Jeff if white people were to blame for racism, which I understood to be a manifestation of human nature. Jeff wasn't interested in blame, but he affirmed both that white people constructed racism and that white people benefit from racism whether we overtly behave as racists or not.

This was stunning information. Racism was not the actions of some "bad people" who were "over there"; it was within me and places I called home. That was devastating. But I was impelled to learn more. Since I was part of the problem, and my people were the cause of it, I felt galvanized to act. I realized it was insufficient to be a passive "nonracist" and I committed to antiracism.

My life since then has revolved around racial justice and equity work. I became involved in activism and community organizing, in my town and among Quakers. In 2008, I began working professionally with CSWAC, where I am now director of training. My interest in feminism fell away almost entirely. I didn't question why.

In the fall of 2018, as the country prepared for the centennial of the 19th amendment, Brent Staples (2018) wrote in the *New York Times* about white suffragists betraying Black womxn who fought for suffrage. I already knew a little about such outrages as white womxn requiring Black suffragists to march at the back of the parade in Washington in 1913. But I didn't know icons like Susan B. Anthony and Elizabeth Cady Stanton had gone on the road to vilify Black men as unqualified for the vote. I was ignorant of most of the Black womxn leaders in the suffrage movement, and I didn't know that once white womxn were enfranchised they turned their backs on the issues of Womxn of Color.

Then I came across Danielle Slaughter's (2018) online article, "The Most Dangerous Person in America Is the White Woman." Slaughter contended white womxn's words and tears have led to the deaths of innumerable People of Color. Because white womxn have been placed at the top of the cult of American womanhood, no one calls them on their power and privilege.

Next, I read Elizabeth Gillespie McRae's (2018) book, *Mothers of Massive Resistance*, which details white womxn's persistent, nationwide organizing for Jim Crow from the 1920s to 1960s. In it, McRae declared white supremacy had been shaped by the "grassroots resistance" of white womxn. Though I had departed from the feminist movement, my identity as a woman was still important to me. My sense of myself as a member of an oppressed group, womxn, was challenged as I learned about the power of white womxn as a bloc. I wanted to know more. If white womxn are so powerful, couldn't we do more to end racism? The book *They Were Her Property: White Women as Slave Owners in the American South* by Jones-Rogers (2019) bowled me over with the extent to which white womxn were not only complicit but architects at the table inventing and building white supremacy.

I knew of course that collusion was not relegated to the past. As I researched the modern womxn's movement, also known as white feminism, I understood why I had left. And I wanted to reclaim my feminist identity, but married with my antiracist self. I decided to create a workshop where white womxn could study our racist history and confront white supremacy embedded in the feminist movement.

DESIGNING THE WORKSHOP

As I deepened my study of white womxn's complicity, I was drawn to two premises. One was that, like white people generally, white womxn operate largely in ignorance of our history, both what we have done well and where we have gone wrong. What happened to us? What forces shaped us? Without knowing where we came from, how can we truly know who we are and where we can go? I wanted to offer a workshop examining white womanhood as a space to construct a possible narrative of white womxn, from the beginning.

Second, I believed white womxn need to know details of our participation in white supremacy culture from the outset. Cultural silence surrounding the role of white womxn in building and maintaining white supremacy is essential for its success. I wanted to learn alongside antiracist partners who would use the education to further our activism.

These premises are captured in the title of the workshop, The Arc of White Womanhood. The arc is our story, and also our aim—to bend toward justice (to borrow from Dr. King). I was fortunate to find a partner in Robin Schlenger. A cis-gender white woman, Robin is also an experienced antiracist trainer who, with a Black co-trainer, leads the workshop Shame Resilience Skills for White People. Robin shared my enthusiasm for examining white feminism and white antiracist womxn. We combined our research and set about planning a workshop. Each of us reached out to colleagues of color; at all times, antiracism work should center the experiences, voices, and issues of BIPOC, and we wanted to proceed with this central tenet in mind. Our goal was not to increase their labor but to ensure space for the thoughts and feedback of BIPOC.

Robin and I agreed the course must present an intellectual education balanced with opportunity for affective processing. Our purpose was to convey painful truths with compassion and humility, and with the aim of empowering and inspiring, rather than paralyzing, blaming, or shaming our participants. We included elements in each session such as body scans, meditations, and break-out rooms to process cognitive, emotional, and somatic responses to course content. We required participants to join small accountability groups that met between sessions to do homework and to provide a compassionate, brave space for the inevitable emotional labor. We emphasized approaching the subject with honesty, courage, empathy, and self-care. White womxn who have fought racism were lifted up as models and inspiration.

We were committed to delivering as much information as possible, while also affording sufficient time for discussion. We restricted lectures to no more than 15 minutes each, sometimes supplemented with slides, videos, or other support materials. Conversation followed, in both small and large groups. For each session we provided a curated list of resources, some required, many optional, for further study. This allowed participants to take in additional information as desired. Resources included a variety of media to accommodate different learning styles.

One other consideration was the audience. We agreed that we desired a caucus space, also known as an affinity group. A caucus is a group gathered around a shared identity, to explore issues specific to that group. (My mother's feminist consciousness-raising group was my first experience of caucusing.) Racial identity affinity groups are a respected strategy in the antiracist community. Robin and I invited white-identified trans womxn and nonbinary people as well as cisgender womxn to our workshop.

Because we inaugurated the course in the fall of 2020 during the COVID-19 pandemic, we designed it to be held virtually in five sessions of 2 hours each. The topics we developed for the five sessions were as follows:

Session 1. The long view: A possible narrative of white womxn
Session 2. A closer view: Architects of white supremacy, and racial justice warriors
Session 3. Intersectionality: Multiplied oppression of Womxn of Color
Session 4. Impacts of white supremacy on white womxn
Session 5. Wholeness

To free ourselves as much as possible to concentrate on delivering the workshop, we traded free enrollment to two womxn who agreed to serve as registrar and technical support.

IMPLEMENTING THE WORKSHOP

Thirty womxn registered for the program, paying approximately $180 each. One participant had to withdraw for health reasons. Most of the others attended most if not all sessions; many stayed for an optional 15-minute Q&A held after each session. Ages ranged from 20s to 70+ years. We did not inquire into gender identities, but based on participants' comments during discussions, there were a few participants who were not cisgender. A wide range of occupations and professions was represented.

My vision was to open the course with a brief but compelling review of the narrative of white womxn. I wanted participants to be grounded in that story, particularly details of trauma that have made a multigenerational impact. We talked in the first session about the origins of humanity in Africa, and migration to Europe beginning about 45,000 years BCE. We invited participants to remember our ancestors, who lived thousands of years ago in comparative peace and equality in a culture that venerated womxn and Goddesses. We reviewed the rise of patriarchy, capitalism, and the Church that destroyed worship of the feminine, murdered millions of womxn in witch hunts, robbed a majority of the population of their land through the enclosure movement, and eventually drove the peasantry across the ocean to another continent.

In Sessions 2 and 3, we studied areas of U.S. history where white womxn played an important role creating and enforcing white supremacy. Like myself, participants had been taught that womxn, for the most part, were innocent bystanders. In actuality, plenty of white womxn enslaved African people, sometimes treating them with great brutality. There was widespread membership in white womxn's chapters of the Ku Klux Klan, and during the anti-busing campaigns of early 1970s, white mothers hurled eggs and the N-word at Black school children. Most womxn in the workshop were unaware of the depth and persistence of racism in every wave of feminism, continuing to the present. Ignorance of womxn's past collusion with white supremacy is due in part to the patriarchy's silencing of womxn's voices and accomplishments. In addition, a favorite strategy of white supremacy culture is to obscure the puppet strings so that systemic racial oppression appears to be the natural order.

In the third session we introduced intersectionality and the multiplied oppression of Womxn of Color (WOC) as targets of racism, sexism, and more. We presented information on health, education, and criminal injustice system issues that plague WOC specifically. Too many white womxn are ignorant of these and other social ills because they don't affect us directly.

Two themes emerged in the early sessions. First, white supremacy culture allots white womxn a status that is both subjugated and privileged. For the most part, white womxn have struck a "deal with the devil" to accept loss of power, resources, and esteem, in exchange for privilege and protection. One example was a comparison of white womxn's status in the early 1800s with the status of Haudenosaunee (Iroquois) womxn. In social, economic, political, and religious spheres, Haudenosaunee womxn commanded respect and authority, where white womxn had few rights. Yet the white womxn had the power and privilege of their whiteness.

A second theme was that white supremacy culture relegates womxn to a singular role as mothers and exploits white womxn *as mothers* to perpetuate and reinforce that culture, idealizing and idolizing motherhood to distract womxn from their loss of power and agency. Much of white womxn's work to build and uphold white supremacy culture has been done in the name of motherhood. For example, white womxn taught their children the business of managing enslaved African people because it was their job as mothers to educate. White segregationists of the early and mid-1900s mounted campaigns to revise textbooks and train teachers in a racist agenda, to protect the education of white children. Antibusing campaigns of the early 1970s invoked motherly duty to white children. In the past few years, white mothers in New York City have erupted in outrage as the city attempted to racially diversify schools.

In the fourth session we posited that white womxn have been "white supremacized" (my term). We looked at two impacts of this process: problematic behaviors stemming from white supremacy, and damage suffered from identification with whiteness over femaleness or other primary identities. Problematic behaviors included white womxn's tears, white savior complex, voting for racist white politicians, seeking relationships with People of Color without regard for racial justice issues, and white womxn policing social spaces. A theme we introduced in this connection is that white womxn are viewed as moral arbiters of U.S. society. Their presumed innocence and virtue are concessions from patriarchal white society to keep them in their place. The damsel role is a source of white womxn's power in white supremacy culture.

Ways that white womxn pay a steep price for the benefits of whiteness include the following:

- Loss of power (social, spiritual, economic, and political)
- Destruction of self-esteem and self-love when our bodies don't conform to white supremacy standards
- Dissociation from emotions and intuitive knowledge disparaged by white culture
- Loss of autonomy as second-class citizens whose work has been devalued
- Profound trauma from generations of oppressing other human beings

These costs are by no means to be compared with the devastating effects of systemic racism on POC. But neither should the damage to white womxn be ignored.

The final session looked at specific complexities faced by white womxn. An example is that white womxn must not hijack racial justice spaces, or center ourselves, with our tears. But white culture teaches us to express many emotions through tears that can be hard to suppress. What does a white antiracist woman do when grief and empathy, or anger, arise in tears? We also spent time in the closing session considering advice from antiracist leaders about how white womxn can use our power and privilege to help society move forward.

Critical Moments of Challenge

Ahistorical and Action Biases. White people are strongly socialized to focus on doing, not processing. We are trained to fix things, preferably immediately. We don't want to waste time learning about them. We also don't want to know about the past. The bias toward action and away from historical education frequently arises in antiracism work. For instance, at our second session, one participant objected. She was frustrated we were spending so much time learning history; she preferred to be in action. The facilitator encouraged her to notice what might be underneath her discomfort, and then moved on. The distress of a white woman works powerfully to derail all else, even in a course designed to interrogate such patterns. Since Robin and I did not sense that other participants were stuck, we chose not to allow this distraction. To our surprise, the participant remained engaged, attending every session thereafter, and rating the workshop highly in her evaluation.

White Fragility. An example of white fragility (see Chapter 1) was the participant who dropped the course after the second session. She explained later that she appreciated the class, but it was "too much." This participant was very new to antiracist work, and it seemed likely the information was overwhelming. Other participants let us know they found the content demanding but were able to stay the course.

Literacy Moments. Several times we interjected a literacy moment to make sure we all shared an understanding of terms. For instance, we pointed out that the term "suffragette" is a pejorative word that was used to belittle those in the womxn's suffrage movement. The label the womxn themselves used was "suffragist." We course leaders were also educated at times. One participant felt we did an inadequate job including people with gender identities other than womxn. Robin and I acknowledged that as cisgender womxn, we have more to learn about gender inclusive language and approaches.

Somatic Dissociation. A prompt we gave regularly for breakout rooms and accountability group homework was "Where is this information landing in your body?" Toward the end of the course, we recognized that many of us have been so trained by white culture to ignore our bodies, it was a struggle to feel somatic impacts at all.

Regaining that faculty is a workshop of its own. Of course, we continued to invite participants to make the attempt.

Overachieving. Robin and I realized by Session 2 that we had been far too ambitious in scheduling lectures. We were learning so much from our research, we felt obligated to share everything with participants. Meanwhile, because much of the information was brand new to our audience, it required more time for processing than we had allowed. We made course corrections as we went along, dropping less critical topics and adding resources for participants to study on their own time, as desired.

Lack of Sources. Our plan to lift up white antiracist sheroes from the past was complicated by the fact that womxn tend to be erased from history, and so do antiracist activists. We succeeded in finding short biographies of at least one or two such people in each of the time periods examined, but more would be desirable.

Decentering, Not Recentering, Whiteness. A challenge that frequently arises in doing antiracism work with white people is how to focus on whiteness while decentering whiteness. We met this challenge imperfectly. For example, at the first session I shared that studying this subject had been deeply meaningful to me personally, as I began to reclaim my full womanity. I was no longer rejecting my feminine self in favor of my antiracist identity. Not till after the session did I realize the implication might be that I was doing this work solely for my own benefit. I opened the second session by recognizing that although I believe white people need to do racial justice work for the sake of our own humanity, this should never take precedence over doing the work for the sake of Indigenous and Black people and People of Color, who are targets of white supremacy every day of their lives. To try to avoid recentering whiteness, we drew on books, articles, videos, and other materials by POC. As mentioned, in Session 3 we raised awareness about some of the specific dilemmas faced by WOC.

No Quick Fix. We had optimistically proposed "Wholeness" as the title of the closing session. However, by the time we arrived at that point, Robin and I were clear there was no wholeness, no solidarity, no neat bow to tie up the program. Although white culture loves an easy fix and a satisfying ending, we had to make do with having engaged a cohort of antiracists in messy, painful work with no end in sight.

Critical Moments of Promise

Personal Growth. Perhaps it will seem narcissistic to open this section by stating that I experienced personal growth in the course of designing and implementing The Arc of White Womanhood. Certainly, the intent of the workshop was to support others in learning and growing. As an educator, I know the process of teaching is most powerful when the teacher is also a learner. I believe it was significant to the success of the workshop that before, during, and after the class, I developed intellectually, emotionally, and spiritually. In particular, I became aware of the extent to which I had discarded the feminist movement because of its embedded racism, and how that had left me without support, opportunities for personal development, and accountability as a female. I was deeply moved to realize I did not need to choose between feminism and antiracism and that in fact the two should be mutually supportive. I experienced this internally as a greater wholeness of self, a self-encompassing of both my womanhood and my antiracism. Externally, it translated into a commitment to work toward a marriage of those two communities. And ultimately, of course, to bring all anti-oppression work under the same roof.

My eyes were opened as well to the degree to which I unconsciously enjoyed my white female privilege, especially an unearned sense of moral superiority. I found that, much as I have already learned about the hardships faced by WOC, I really know only the tip of the iceberg. Expressing these and other growth points in the workshop served as a model for participants, many of whom shared similar growing edges.

Partnership. Creating partnership with Robin Schlenger was a huge gift of this workshop. We quickly developed a deep trust and friendship that made it easy to design the program together. We leaned on each other as we waded into very painful stories of white womxn's treachery, and our own failings as white womxn. Robin's research, expertise, and insights complemented mine, resulting in an impactful workshop design. White supremacy culture often divides white people not only from POC but from each other. In the antiracist community, white people often compete to be the "best white ally in the room" or otherwise distance from other white people. It is no small matter when two white folks form a strong and lasting relationship in an antiracist context.

Brave Space. The Robins, as we were nicknamed, also led the workshop in complementary fashion. Robin S. tended more toward the emotional, and I leaned a bit more toward the academic. Both of us demonstrated humility, openness, compassion, and vulnerability. This created a safe, inviting space where participants could share deeply, and constructively challenge themselves and each other.

Connection. In the first session, I evoked Europeans thousands of years ago as our ancestors—people we may never think about or know anything about, yet to whom we are intimately connected. Many white people suffer from an unconscious feeling of hollowness or rootlessness, because our culture, unlike some, dismisses the importance of history, including personal heritage. Participants expressed deep appreciation for recovering a sense of ancient ancestors. We referred interested womxn to courses the organization White Awake offers on deep exploration of European roots.

Analysis. As a result of the workshop, one participant realized that "in the lives of Black people, in particular, we white womxn actually function as an armed patrol in the white supremacy surveillance system." Another observed that patriarchy and white supremacy are not separate systems but go hand in hand. A third person was able to share with a friend the insights about white silence that she gained in our course. It was rewarding to see such light bulbs going off throughout the program.

Solidarity. A theme we returned to many times was that white womxn are impacted by a mix of privilege and oppression. We asked how we can leverage our power in service to racial justice and equity. The perspective that white womxn have explicit power in a racialized society will inform our actions and approaches. The recognition that white supremacy culture punishes us even as it accords some privilege affected participants deeply. This analysis may lead white womxn to seek to act in solidarity with POC rather than always investing in whiteness.

In addition, education about specific challenges faced by WOC due to intersecting oppressions opened eyes. Participants left the workshop inspired to address issues of Black and Brown girls and womxn.

Commitment. As of this writing, some of the accountability groups continue to meet. Participants found the material and analysis presented in the course compelling, and the structure of accountability groups was found to suit carrying the exploration further.

RECOMMENDATIONS AND VISIONS

In planning for a next round of the workshop, the Robins agreed it should be lengthier. More spaciousness was needed for large and small group conversation to process so much complex and disturbing information. There is also much more content to offer, but we felt that would have to wait for a more advanced workshop. We agreed to repeat the original course, expanded to seven 2-hour sessions.

Clearer communication about and to the intended audience is needed. As cisgender womxn, Robin and I both need reminders not to address everyone in the workshop as "womxn," since not all participants identify as such. We will improve language of gender inclusivity both in promotional materials and in the sessions.

The experience of the newcomer who found the class too painful and demanding suggests we might consider recommending that only people who have done some antiracist work already should participate. Meanwhile, we secured permission to share with participants a short paper, "Teach Us to Sit Still: Coming Home after the Undoing Racism Workshop," by Frank and Golden (2012). The authors address that premature urge felt by many new antiracists to move directly into action without first doing the homework.

The goal of exploring examples of white womxn's involvement in multiracial antiracist coalitions was not met in the fall course, partly due to lack of time. In expanding the workshop to seven sessions, we plan to dedicate time for this topic.

We are considering the possibility of recording an on-demand version of The Arc of White Womanhood. Tapes could then be viewed by people who can't commit the time or money to the live course, or who do not fit our target audience.

For a future undertaking, we would be interested in facilitating a seminar for graduates of The Arc of White Womanhood, who would conduct research into antiracist activism by white womxn past and present, perhaps producing papers or an edited book on this subject.

CONCLUSION

While white men have generally been viewed as the top of the oppressor heap, white womxn are much closer to the top than I had ever realized. Though we have suffered under patriarchy, white womxn have thrown ourselves mind, body, and soul into the project of sealing white supremacy culture so we can reap its benefits, at the expense of People of Color.

Multiracial antiracist community offers a much healthier life for all. The more we educate white womxn about our part in the intersecting oppressions that hold humanity down, the more likely we are to recognize that our deal with white supremacy and patriarchy costs too much. There are far more rewarding deals to be made.

REFERENCES

Frank, P. B., & Golden, G. (2012). Teach us to sit still: Coming home after the undoing racism workshop. *National Organization for Men against Racism.* Accessed on January 10, 2022, from https://nomas.org/teach-us-to-sit-still-coming-home-after-the-undoing-racism-workshop.

Gillespie McRae, E. (2018). *Mothers of massive resistance: White women and the politics of white supremacy.* Oxford University Press.

Jones-Rogers, S. (2019). *They were her property: White women as slave owners in the American South.* Yale University Press.

Slaughter, D. (2018). The most dangerous person in America is the white woman. *Mamademics.* Accessed on January 10, 2022, from http://mamademics.com/the-most-dangerous-person-in-america-is-the-white-woman.

Staples, B. (2018, July 28). How the suffrage movement betrayed Black women. *New York Times.* Accessed on January 10, 2022, from https://www.nytimes.com/2018/07/28/opinion/sunday/suffrage-movement-racism-black-women.html.

Part III

LESSONS LEARNED AND CHALLENGES AHEAD

In this part, the chapter authors share what they learned as co-directors and as facilitators for RISE for Racial Justice. We intend for this part to provide an approach/blueprint for how one might engage in similar work without a prescriptive "how to" approach. We emphasize that this work must be localized and temporal, although we resist notions of doing this work in only physical communities given that much of 2020–2021 was spent being together in communities that were virtual.

Chapter 9 discusses how identities and subjectivities, those of facilitators and participants, inform the spaces created and the work that is possible. Chapter 10 examines the realities of the tensions of teaching politically charged material with a focus on the history of the development of a new course, How to Talk About Palestine. Finally, Chapter 11 reviews how RISE for Racial Justice adjusted from a small-scale to a larger organization serving 10 times as many participants. This chapter takes on the uncomfortable conversations about attending to logistics, compensation, and a "common curriculum." We acknowledge and strongly suggest in these chapters that facilitators and creators of similar programs be attentive to the needs of their particular communities when they design and implement courses.

CHAPTER 9

Understanding Black Resistance to Antiracist Work
The Sonia Syndrome

Kimberly Williams Brown

This chapter grows out of my work with cross-racial dialogue among K–12 teachers in a public-school district in New York. Over 25 teachers joined the course and we divided them into three smaller sections so that we could create more intimate and personal learning experiences. I taught this course with an interracial team of six facilitators; we assigned two members of the team to each of the sections.

As we prepared together for this dialogue among K–12 teachers, we wanted to make sure that Teachers of Color were not divided across the six sessions such that a Teacher of Color would be the "only" in any section. We were working with teachers from a predominantly white, conservative school district where Teachers of Color make up about 6% of the population according to the school district's website; so our efforts to make sure teachers were not isolated were sometimes difficult, but especially necessary in this district.

Sonia, a West Indian Black womxn who enrolled in this course, was one of only two BIPOC participants who signed up. My own work with Afro-Caribbean teachers (Williams Brown, 2021) and how they come to understand race immediately made alarm bells go off for me. I have been facilitating intergroup dialogue for about 16 years and my research to date has focused on Afro-Caribbean womxn teachers' experiences with race/racism in the United States. The ways in which Afro-Caribbean people navigate their colonial histories can be quite different from the way African American people do. Although Sonia was not assigned to my section of the course, she played a central role in our team planning meetings over the 6 weeks that we taught the course.

In our facilitation model, we follow the Intergroup Dialogue approach to co-facilitation (see Chapter 2). We are attentive to identities and try to pair facilitators who identify across a variety of social indicators (Zúñiga et al., 2014). We emphasize particular identities that demonstrate the subject of the dialogue. For example, if the dialogue is about race, which in our case all the dialogues are, we pair a white facilitator and a Facilitator of Color together while being attentive to other dynamics of power, including but not limited to gender, class, caste, and (dis)ability. The Facilitator of Color assigned to this section was triggered by Sonia every week because Sonia refused to see how race and racism were structural and how race and racism differently affected white people (advantaging them without merit) and People of Color (disadvantaging them without cause). In fact, Sonia was intent on upholding white superiority.

I had seen these dynamics in my own family and Afro-Caribbean friend groups. As an Afro-Jamaican living in the United States for 22 years, I recognized in Sonia some of the dynamics I had experienced or seen over time. Race and racism were not always as obvious to me as they are now. Some of the subtleties of white supremacy evaded me until I learned of the histories of settler colonialism (see Wolfe, 1999); racial hierarchies; institutional racism through red lining (Kreiger et al., 2020), policing, and police structures; the aftermath of *Brown v. Board of Education*; and the emergence of critical race theory (CRT) from legal scholars responding to racism in the legal system. I have also been deeply influenced by feminist thinking and in particular decolonial, transnational, and Black and Caribbean feminisms that speak deeply to both my intellectual projects and how I show up in the world. To think with scholars and theorists who are a part of these traditions has allowed me to do what Love and Muhammad (2017) call us to do in spaces of dialogue when we are deeply triggered by those who look like us but are ideologically far removed from our experiences. They ask that we be intentional about words, that we are careful about how we respond so we can teach and model for everyone how to respond.

It is with this advice in mind that I led our group of facilitators into thinking about what would be a useful way to respond to Sonia as well as to Black people and People of Color we know who continue to uphold white supremacy. To date, little has been written that specifically addresses how we do this; what follows below is not a prescriptive solution but an approach that allows us to teach and facilitate without traumatizing POC or reinforcing dangerous stereotypes and tropes for white people. As explained in Chapter 1, Robin DiAngelo's (2018) *White Fragility* provides an approach to understanding how white supremacy circulates in everyday situations for many white people. Below, drawing on my 16 years of facilitating, I propose a way to think about how some Black people uphold white supremacy and what we may do to better navigate the spaces in which we find ourselves with them.

THE SONIA SYNDROME

I use the phrase "The Sonia Syndrome" to describe a Black person who was not born in the United States but now resides and works here. This person has spent a portion (at least 5 years) of their adult life navigating systems and processes that are situated outside of the United States. They have also spent a portion of time (at least 5 years) navigating systems in the United States.

First, many readers may wonder how a Black person living in the United States could possibly uphold white supremacy. It seems antithetical to the historical legacies of the foundations of the country, the constitution, and the genocide we know that took place here. Sonia Syndrome describes a Black person who epitomizes being pro-white, with pro-white thought and pro-white ways of life. Being pro-white does not have to be negative, but when that person is also anti-Black people, anti-Black thought, and anti-Black ways of life, then we have to address why white is always right or in this case, always better. In other words, this approach must be picked apart and understood for what it is. There are no neutral ways of understanding the world.

Such people have been called derogatory terms such as "Oreo," referencing the popular snack in its original state, which is black on the outside but white on the inside. Name calling has never been useful or helpful in understanding how we navigate conversations in our personal lives or in interracial dialogic spaces. If we want to understand better what allows a person to be anti-Black when they themselves are Black, we must realize and theorize the qualities and ways of being in the world that are common to such people. We must then understand what might be helpful as a way out for them. We must also know when to walk away because racial battle fatigue (Smith, 2014) takes a toll on all of us (see also Chapter 1). In the following sections I will examine the key reasons that (Black) people hold fast to white supremacist ideologies:

1. Ahistorical ideas
2. A belief that individual bad actors commit bad acts
3. A clash between individuated identity and the politics of identity
4. A fear of a shifting sense of self

Ahistorical Ideas

As a Black immigrant, I hear people in my communities often repeating harmful stereotypes and tropes about Black people without knowing where they come from, understanding them, or making any attempt to debunk them. This phenomenon appears to be mostly true in immigrant circles, but if one looks closely, one will notice it as well in Black people born and raised in the United States. So, we cannot be content to say it's merely the ignorance of "foreigners" without exploring how people who live in this country also make these claims.

The first reason is that when people have not otherwise challenged the histories readily available in schools about U.S. and world history, they hold fast to false claims about white freedom and Black unfreedom. People who have an ahistorical view often think that slavery is only historical, with no bearing on our present and our future. The same is true for colonialism. Colonialism becomes a thing of the past and all the economic and political struggles of countries in the global south or the countries once colonized are individual failures because the governments are corrupt or lazy. Wolfe (1999), leading scholar on settler colonialism, astutely notes that settler colonialism is a structure and not an event. Ahistoricizing events allows people to miss the structures that connect them to the present and to the future. For example, thinking that slavery is perpetually in the past does not allow people to see how slavery is directly connected to prisons, gentrification, and "failing" schools, issues that plague us today.

In 1977 the statement issued by the Combahee River Collective gave us a road map, a structure, for understanding the multiply marginalized (Combahee River Collective, 2014). That made it possible for Crenshaw (1990) to coin the word "intersectionality" to describe how the structures and systems of oppression create disadvantage/poverty and inequality for some people. Without an understanding of these forces and structures working together in deliberate and sometimes unintentional ways to create injustice, some immigrants to America as well as some native-born may be unaware of those processes. It can take years of reading critical theories and learning to see the world differently—to begin making connections across these structures.

When working with Black people or other People of Color who insist on resisting an antiracist curriculum, it is important to understand how they think ahistorically and their connections to the present and the future. Knowing this will give us a place as facilitators from which to focus our work with them. This may mean introducing readings, as well as creating break-out groups that address specific questions that target this thinking and lack of awareness.

As facilitators, it means that we must be aware of our histories of racism, colonialism, and settler colonialism. Without such an understanding, it is not possible for us to make connections for the Sonia's in our sessions. When a white person resists in this way in our dialogue sessions, we often pull from people like Kivel (2011), who discusses in detail the costs of racism to white people, or DiAngelo (2018), who discusses the fragility of whiteness and white people. Yet those resources have not been similarly synthesized and historicized for Black people or People of Color because we often assume that Black people must understand racism and always come with complex understandings of systems and structures. None of this is true. Black people and other People of Color are also learning and unlearning history, processing experiences that have happened to them and trying to live in ways that are not about how others see them through a deficit frame.

A Belief That Individual Bad Actors Commit Bad Acts

The Sonia Syndrome can also stem from a belief that all people are basically good although some people are all bad. The tendency of those experiencing the Sonia Syndrome to ahistoricize events works hand-in-hand with a tendency to believe that all people are good or have good intentions while acknowledging that there are a few "bad apples." This tendency relegates to the past colonialism, settler colonialism, slavery, imperialism, and other atrocities without taking into account structures and systems that continue to uphold these kinds of acts. People with the Sonia Syndrome tend to buy into the idea that people are inherently good and therefore could never be racist because racism and race are experienced on an individual rather than a collective level. Again, this is rooted in lack of recognition of any collective experience that would allow these individuals to make sense of racialization.

It may seem easier to believe that events like colonization, the Holocaust, and other genocides were a result of individual actors and not a collective effort steeped in ideas of difference, purity, and hierarchy. People experiencing the Sonia Syndrome firmly believe that if individuals like Oprah Winfrey and Barack Obama can "make" it, then all Black people can also make it by individual effort. There is no accounting, for instance, for the systematic ways in which race, poverty, policing, and schooling are tied together in such intricate ways that few children make it to elite colleges from high-need high schools despite ability. This, of course, is in stark contrast to the higher percentage of children who will attend elite colleges because their high schools were well-resourced.

Thus, the inability to see that individuals are part of collective wealth, racial, and gender systems produces the Sonia Syndrome. Recently, I have been watching footage of Black people in public spaces disagreeing loudly with critical race theory. One was a doctor who said, "I made it through college and have a medical degree. How did 'the man' hold me back?" If one gets caught in this argument, one would find herself confused if she did not understand that 5.4% of the total doctors in the United States are Black, while, in 2018, 13% of the U.S. population was Black (Alt, 2021). The attention-grabbing headline of Alt's article, "Percentage of Doctors Who are Black, Barely Changed in 120 years," speaks volumes. To look at individual cases is to tell a small part of the story that evades the truth of systemic injustice and oppression and all the ways in which oppressions interlock to create complex systems of injustice. This point of view is associated with the next tendency of individuals experiencing the Sonia Syndrome.

A Clash Between Individuated Identity and the Politics of Identity

When identity is individuated, and not thought of as social, then we homogenize experiences in dangerous ways. This process of homogenization can create camps that reduce the beauty and diversity of identity into caricatures and stereotypes. Identity politics dictate how members of social groups should act and creates a universalizing effect. Critics of identity politics such as Mollow (2004), Gimenez (2006), and Gitlin (2020), for example, argue that identity politics silences particular identities such as class and disability, while it subverts the need for insurgency and the demand for representation. From the

1970s through the 1990s, when theories of identity politics arose out of the Civil Rights Movement, the Stonewall era, and the Disability Rights Movement, there was a strong pull to politicize identities so as to create coalitional resistance and not individual resistance. To some degree, we have lost the political and radical roots of these early movements. They were not just simply about representation but were about conscious representation to debunk the myths of eugenics, separate-but-equal, and that failure to thrive rested squarely on the shoulders of individuals. The radical imaginings of a just, nonhierarchical world have today become about individual achievement, representation for the sake of diversity, and a watered-down policing of individual ways of making sense of lived and intersectional identities.

Because we lost sight of the real lesson of these radical political movements, we are not always clear about how identity is co-created and our responsibilities to each other. People experiencing the Sonia Syndrome with a more individuated identity do not have a way to imagine themselves with the radical potential of being a part of a political movement connected to their identities. That dislocates them from being able to co-construct meaning about their racial identity. In other words, they may feel that they have to accept derogatory ideas about Blackness or, in some cases, reject Blackness altogether. Furthermore, the possibility for coalition across diverse identities is lost for those committed to an individuated sense of self.

Two tools that have been used to address diversity and identity politics on a federal and scholarly level are affirmative action and multipartiality, often misunderstood as unfair practices that exclude or limit white people from access to college admissions, workplaces, and other entities. Of course, affirmative action is not this simplified tool of exclusion but is instead an approach that attempts to close the hierarchical gap between those with privileged identities and those with marginalized identities. In 1965, when the Affirmative Action Executive Order was issued (see Rubenfeld, 1997), the goal and intent was to provide equitable access to work for People of Color and womxn. It was not intended to become a weaponized political tool, because, at its inception, right after the Civil Rights legislation, it was obvious that there needed to be a systematic way of reducing discrimination for groups that had been disenfranchised and not afforded access to institutions and spaces because of gender or race for decades. Affirmative action has traveled beyond the workplace and has had case precedence in higher education (with the University of Michigan's affirmative action case being the most famous example [Gurin et al., 2004]). In the case of *Gratz v. Bolinger*, there was a challenge to college admissions on the grounds of diversity diluting the academic profile and rigor of institutions of higher education. The University of Michigan won both suits brought against it because it had a rich history of diversity and dialogue and inclusive policies. Helping people experiencing the Sonia Syndrome understand these legal histories can open up ways of thinking about their own identity to admit the power of collective identity and the power of resisting colonial narratives.

Facilitators of dialogue can introduce participants to multipartiality. Multipartiality, also developed at the University of Michigan through its Intergroup Relations program, "is a power-balancing approach to Intergroup Dialogue that supports and sustains all voices, especially the minoritized voices or the concerns and needs of those with less power" (Fisher & Petryk, 2017). In the dialogues we facilitate, we are careful to employ multipartiality as part of our practice. In many of the school districts and other communities in which we facilitate, the participants are predominantly white. We, therefore, are attentive to the power differences by never placing individual People of Color in break-out groups alone, and we especially never ask them to speak on behalf of a group.

In trainings and workshops about equity, contextualizing and historizing these legal and social mechanisms is important not only for participants displaying the Sonia Syndrome but for all participants as a reminder of the multiplicity of ways in which we need to respond to dialogic spaces. These two are just approaches to addressing individuated identity and the politics of identity. Part of what the history of affirmative action, for example, teaches is that it is possible for the government through legislation to respond to issues of disparity in social identity such as race. Discussing systems though brings its own difficulties.

In many of our trainings and workshops we point to the illusive "system" that is the harbinger of inequity. To Black people who have grown up with government systems that are run by Black people—as is the case in Jamaica and Sierra Leon, just to give two examples—the system is them. They therefore experience a disconnect with the idea that the system is at fault. Now, we can pull this argument apart quite easily by asserting that the system is *them* because the system is the people who make it up and implement policy and structure. There is no neutral machine working to create inequitable structures. It is people who do this. It is also true that the idea that the system is *them* is deeply uncomfortable for the people who have the greatest proximity to power. This is why people are similarly uncomfortable about being named as problematic because whiteness names you as powerful even as it pretends this power has no true effect. While white people and Black people are positioned differently, Black people from majority Black nation-states are acutely aware of not just race differentials in the system but class differentials.

It is therefore prudent, as we set up antiracist workshops and spaces, that we know our audience to be able to provide broader examples of systemic structures that one can use to approximate structures of whiteness and racism in the United States. While there is no hierarchy of oppression (Lorde, 1983), race in the United States functions differently than most other oppressive systems. The foundations of the United States—first on race through indigenous genocide, Black chattel slavery, and Mexican border erasure—has been immortalized through the Constitution, which made all nonwhite people nonhuman. Because this is how the United States came to be and is still largely experienced by the racialized "other," the "system" must be explained through history, context, and the ways in which laws, processes, and structures work to continue the racial divide that is foundational to the United States as a settler nation-state. In our experience, trainings and workshops often begin with the assumption that everyone is American born, with the same access to history and curriculum. If we begin to experience these spaces as global, we will be better equipped to assist those experiencing the Sonia Syndrome as well as those who are in denial or grew up sheltered and privileged in the United States. The utility of a transnational feminist praxis is that it reminds us that "there is here, and here is there." What this means is that I have met many BIPOC Americans who did not quite "get" race and racial politics because to live in a body racialized as inferior is not always to know how this impacts a person intimately. Colonization as a structuring event has fought a valiant fight to dehistoricize the colonizing mission and the violence it takes to continue to subjugate nonwhite people.

A Fear of a Shifting Sense of Self

To be racialized as inferior is shocking when one has always thought of themselves as fully human. This way of understanding the causes of the Sonia Syndrome is informed by Afropessimism. As Wilderson (2020) claims, Afropessimism allows one a wider spectrum of emotions and feelings beyond the structured "feel good" ones we think make us civilized. Afropessimism theorizes from a place of naming the social status assigned to us as "non-human beings." It is social death according to its believers. This social death is what Afro-Caribbeans run from when they come to the United States. Wilderson's work has been severely critiqued by Wekker (2021), who astutely and humorously points out that Wildersons's work is "unloving, hopeless, contradictory, and hypocritical" (p. 95.) What Wekker articulates here is Wilderson's unwillingness to apply an intersectional framework to Blackness. His interpretation and Afropessimism assume that blackness is constructed the same everywhere or that an American, Western understanding of Blackness is applicable as universal to the Black diaspora. This critique expands therefore and mitigates Wilderson's Afropessimism as central to understanding Blackness, so I invoke it here as one reason why people may distance from Blackness.

Afropessimism allows us a lens through which to begin to see that what appears to be anti-Black racism may be a reaction of fear of being labeled as inferior. For some people, to accept that racism exists and that it rests on one's body is to admit that one is seen as inferior even if one does not believe this to be true. So, a distancing from Blackness begins to happen. This distancing is dangerous because one of course cannot distance from one's Black skin. What happens therefore is that people distance from Black culture and wrongfully assume that this will mean greater coherence to the white gaze.

While Afropessimism is important to think with, because it provides a structure or a methodology through which to understand Blackness as social death, it provides an entry point for us to empathize with why people of Afro descent may be hesitant to embrace Blackness. Because racism structures so much of people's lives, and the hurt of it is so insidious, trying to understand it without proper supports in place can break one's will. How do people feel all the pain of racism and still survive? How do they create spaces of love and coherence that have nothing to do with the white gaze? We embrace the pain of racism by dealing with it through therapy and in dialogue spaces as a community. Racial affinity groups (King, 2018) are important for that reason. We can remind participants of the contradiction: that embracing the pain assuages the guilt and, by extension, the exhaustion we feel from anti-Blackness. We must do this in communities of care.

Wilderson's work (2020) should remind facilitators to be fully equipped with nuanced understandings of how Blackness is constructed. The assumption that Black is already inferior, already social death and so the cultures that arise from the diaspora will never be appreciated in the ways that they should be falls short of how Black people across the diaspora experience racialization. This assumption also misses the nuances of how various cultures are defined and operate. In this case, facilitators must be careful not to miss how Blackness across the diaspora is agential, full of life, and mitigated by/cohered with other identities such as class, gender, and ability to produce a Black subject that is more than their Blackness and whose culture is not reducible to caricature elements.

For facilitators who engage in antiracist work, it is paramount that we understand these nuances of anti-Blackness as we respond to the participants in our sessions. We cannot hold space for anti-Black sentiment from white people in the same way that we hold space for anti-Black sentiment from Black people. The histories that create antiracism are different for both groups and need to be responded to in different, nuanced ways.

CRITICAL CEMENTING EVENT

Finally, facilitators can create dialogue with Black participants who display anti-Black sentiment by asking them in racial affinity spaces to relay a moment that has shaped how they think about racism and how they make sense of anti-Black sentiment. A critical cementing event is one that takes place for people that is cumulatively generated but temporally situated. For example, in conversations with Black immigrant faculty recently, we discussed the moment when our consciousness of race as an organizing principle was raised. Some of us cited the 2012 murder of Trayvon Martin. Older ones of us thought of the 1991 Rodney King beating that sparked protests in Los Angeles. And still others named the 2014 murder of Michael Brown as the moment. What each of our stories exposed is that there is an event that takes place that puts into perspective our personal histories with racial discrimination, and the national and structural violence against Black bodies. These histories and national discourses coalesce in a moment for most of us that raise our critical consciousness. We can, in those moments, tease apart what racial violence has done to our understanding of self in ways that were not possible before. It was not possible before because the psychological terror of immigration processes and experiences, or poverty, or the fear of shifting our sense of who we are creates a critical cementing event. As facilitators, we can aid participants in their coming to racial consciousness around these critical cementing events by recognizing the four key reasons why Black people may have anti-Black sentiment and helping them work through moments that become critical cementing events. We can help them feel less alone in this process of coming to critical consciousness, which can often feel like moments of dissonance.

CONCLUSION

As facilitators, we hold much power in our dialogic spaces to shift participants' understanding of the world in vital ways. Anti-Black sentiment from anyone regardless of race is always problematic and should always be addressed quickly and thoughtfully. This requires that as facilitators we recognize the dynamics of anti-Black racism and that we are specific in addressing these issues. At the same time, BIPOC facilitators must also be attentive to themselves and to the multiple histories of violence and trauma we also bring to the spaces we create. How we attend to ourselves will let us know if we have the capacity to attend to Black participants exhibiting anti-Black sentiments.

REFERENCES

Alt, A. (2021, April 21). Percentage of doctors who are Black, barely changed in 120 years. *Medscape Medical Journal*. Retrieved January 10, 2022, from https://www.medscape.com/viewarticle/949673#:~:text=In%20 1940%2C%202.8%25%20of%20physicians,Journal%20of%20 General%20Internal%20Medicine.

Brown, K. W. (2021, January 22). Diasporic Transnationalism, Gender, and Education. In *Oxford Research Encyclopedia of Education*. Oxford University Press.

Combahee River Collective. (2014). A Black Feminist Statement. *Women's Studies Quarterly, 42*(3/4), 271–280. http://www.jstor.org/stable/24365010.

Crenshaw, K. (1991). Mapping the margins: Intersectionality, identity politics, and violence against women of color. *Stanford Law Review, 43*(6), 1241–1300.

DiAngelo, R. (2018). *White fragility: Why it's so hard for white people to talk about racism*. Beacon Press.

Fisher, R., & Petryk, T. (2017). Balancing asymmetrical social power dynamics. *University of Michigan Program on Intergroup Relations Working Paper Series*. Accessed on September 6, 2019, from https://igr.umich.edu /working-paper-series.

Gimenez, M. E. (2006). With a little class: A critique of identity politics. *Ethnicities, 6*(3), 423–439.

Gitlin, T. (2020). The rise of "identity politics": An examination and a critique. In *Higher education under fire* (pp. 308–325). Routledge.

Gurin, P., Lehman, J. S., Lewis, E., Lewis, P. E., Dey, E. L., Hurtado, S., & Gurin, G. (2004). *Defending diversity: Affirmative action at the University of Michigan.* University of Michigan Press.

King, R. (2018). *Mindful of race: Transforming racism from the inside out.* Sounds True.

Kivel, P. (2011). *Uprooting racism: How white people can work for racial justice* (3rd ed.). New Society Publishers.

Krieger, N., Van Wye, G., Huynh, M., Waterman, P. D., Maduro, G., Li, W., Gwynn, R. C., Barbot, O., & Bassett, M. T. (2020). Structural racism, historical redlining, and risk of preterm birth in New York City, 2013–2017. *American Journal of Public Health, 110*(7), 1046–1053.

Lorde, A. (1983). There is no hierarchy of oppressions. *Bulletin: Homophobia and Education, 14*(3/4), 9.

Love, B., & Muhammad, G. E. (2017). Critical community conversations: Cultivating the elusive dialogue about racism with parents, community members, and teachers. *The Educational Forum, 81,* 1–4.

Mollow, A. (2004). Identity politics and disability studies: A critique of recent theory. *Michigan Quarterly Review, 43*(2).

Rubenfeld, J. (1997). Affirmative action. *Yale Law Journal, 107*(8), 427–472.

Smith, W. A. (2014). *Racial battle fatigue in higher education: Exposing the myth of post-racial America.* Rowman & Littlefield.

Wekker, G. (2021). Afropessimism. *European Journal of Women's Studies, 28*(1), 86–97.

Wilderson III, F. B. (2020). *Afropessimism.* Liveright Publishing Corporation.

Wolfe, P. (1999). *Settler colonialism.* A&C Black.

Zúñiga, X., Lopez, G., & Ford, K. A. (2014). *Intergroup dialogue: Engaging difference, social identities, and social justice.* Routledge.

CHAPTER 10

How to Talk About Palestine
Political Contentiousness in Antiracism Training

Nama Khalil and Sarah Moss Yanuck

We designed the course How to Talk About Palestine (HTAP) in response to the 2021 Israeli attacks on Gaza and Palestinians throughout occupied Palestine. At the time, we were facilitating the introductory RISE for Racial Justice course, How to Talk About Racism (HTAR), and we wanted to acknowledge the violence and displacement of Palestinians in our classes, but we were told that doing so would put our colleagues and our organization at risk. This left us feeling frustrated and torn. For Sarah Moss, stories of K–12 teachers being fired for their solidarity with Palestine left her feeling hesitant to act in ways that could jeopardize her and her colleagues. Nama had to reckon with what it might mean to be silenced by suppressing parts of her identity. Staying silent about Palestine felt like compromising our integrity and responsibility as antiracist educators, so we joined efforts and co-dreamed this course together.

OUR JOURNEYS TO ANTIRACISM WORK AND TO EACH OTHER

Nama

I am a child of immigrants who left everything they held dear in Egypt in the hopes of providing a better life for themselves, and better educational opportunities for their future children. I lived a double-conscious life. My days were split between school and home. My school was predominately white, and I was the *only* head-scarf-wearing Muslim to roam the halls, which made me the sole representative of all things Islam and Middle East related—a burden I did not choose.

Our home was an insular, Muslim, Egyptian household: a fragrant mixture of onions and cinnamon would greet anyone at the door, Al Husary's Qur'anic recitation echoed in the early morning, and news from Al-jazeera Arabic broadcasted in the evenings. News about the escalating violence of the Israeli occupation of Palestine, which led to the Second Intifada in 2000, and the lack of aid from neighboring Arab countries consumed my parents. One evening, Baba looked at us and shared a verse from the Qur'an that recounts how justice is central in our faith and how activism is sacred. We discussed the ways that our Prophetic tradition revolved around eradicating injustices. This led to a conversation about how there is an intentional effort in the United States to turn Islam into a spiritual practice void of its anti-oppressive mission. Baba emphasized needing to "begin with ourselves"—we have to be the change we want to see. I carry this value with me today.

After 9/11 and the rise of anti-Muslim racism, there was a clear shift in my parents' support for activism: Baba told us time and again that "this country is not meant for us" and that "we are guests here" so we "have to act accordingly." My parents were adamant that I put my head down and study hard. Baba believed that doing well in school and succeeding professionally were the only ways we would be accepted. They were afraid; how could they not be, when our local imam was stripped from his citizenship and deported for supporting Palestine? FBI surveillance in our community not only harmed us, but divided us, too.

I complied, but it was frustrating to be "the good student" when I encountered racism at school. Students asked me to explain why "they" hate "us." Teachers claimed that Palestinians were terrorists, told me I should not criticize the Iraq war, and joked at my expense that Muslims "blow things up" (a pun shared in photography class where students are told to "blow it up" when enlarging an image). I was confused and felt utterly defeated.

College was different in that I found a way to express myself, but I was still tokenized and othered. I used art as a means of talking back to the silencing I faced in my Muslim community and the anti-Muslim racism I faced in broader society. I spent a lot of my time in our college library, trying to learn from those before me on how to use my craft to make a difference; I wanted to find ways to *act* outside traditional campus organizing. I found inspiration in the works of Emory Douglas, Gordon Parks, and Jones Hogu, artists who helped me become aware of anti-Blackness. I strived to make artwork that invited people to *think*, ask questions, and talk. My research on art and justice led me to readings by Cornel West and Angela Davis. I started to slowly make connections between national and global liberatory movements and was thirsty for more, but I was not clear on what to do next.

As life progressed, I got married, completed a doctoral program, and became a mother. Mothering a newborn during the 45th presidency gave me a lot of angst. I constantly worried about my daughter's sense of belonging, security, and identity. How do I raise my daughter to be confident, empowered, and independent in a society that might not accept her for who she is, a Muslim American? What can I do to make society better for her? This worry solidified when she came home expressing her desire to "be white like Avery," and wanting to "have straight hair, not curly hair." Feeling sad and ill-equipped to address this with her teachers, I signed up for HTAR with RISE for Racial Justice. Explicitly naming race and unpacking it from a personal and institutional perspective made everything—my confusion, my anger, my helplessness, my experiences, my fears, my artwork, my studies—make sense. I felt empowered. With a new sense of purpose, language, and grounding in antiracism work, I asked to join their facilitation team. It was here that I met Sarah Moss and our journeys converged.

Sarah Moss

I grew up in a white, Ashkenazi Jewish family in a university town in North Carolina, where in many ways my family mirrored the white liberal culture around us. There were two aspects of my family, though, that became integral ingredients of my race work: our Jewishness and an unusually high frequency of dialogue within our family.

Being Jewish in my family meant many things—Passover at Grandma and Grandpa's house, hating Hebrew School but loving my Bat Mitzvah, endless Jewish humor, and stories. From the time I was a small child, adults told stories of antisemitic persecution. They told stories of pogroms that most—but not all—of Nana's siblings escaped, and stories of when Great-Grandpa Hoffie suddenly stopped receiving letters from his parents and siblings in Austria in 1941. Alternating generations either never mentioned or constantly talked about antisemitic violence, but the trauma was a consistent presence. Growing up as a white child in the suburbs, my own experience was far from the violence my grandparents and great-grandparents knew, but the history was alive in both what we talked about and what we avoided.

We talked often about interpersonal conflict. I learned dialogue in my family long before I knew it had a name. Countless times, my parents, my brother, and I sat in the living room to talk through a conflict. There was nothing perfect about the fights that led us to the living room or about the reparative conversations that followed, but I did learn from a young age that difficult conversations can lead to deeper understanding and to new possibilities in relationships. I learned that conflict is survivable, common, and can be engaged with care.

In college, learning about environmental racism and genocides that I had never heard of disrupted my sense of the world. I began to reckon with my own role in perpetuating racist systems. In the midst of this learning, a friend of mine from high school died suddenly. Something fractured in me when she died. In "Healing Is Rhizomatic: A Conceptual Framework and Tool," Lopez (2020) describes "fracture" as "breaking and separation that impacts our state and capacity to be and grow as we once were and did." She explains:

> Fractures can be immensely and intensely painful. They can break us in ways that are irreparable, make us lose things that we cannot recover. Fractures, when understood in the context of rhizomatic growth, can also create new contexts. In that way, they can facilitate flow and growth in multiple directions and make other connections, fractures, and blockages possible. (p. 5)

My fracture layered with the ways my sense of the world was disrupted as I learned more about race. I'm not sure how deeply I would have engaged with race if I weren't already feeling cracked open—if the emotional comfort I was accustomed to wasn't already so disarrayed. The death of my friend and my introduction to antiracism also took me outside the comfort zones of those I had previously counted on; my relationships began to fracture, too. I was seeing racism in and around me. I was grieving. I was hungry for analyses that could help me make sense of the world, practices that would help me engage well, and relationships where people turned toward difficult conversations and were willing to get real.

I found the beginning of such analyses, practices, and relationships in my education classes. One class in particular, Pedagogies of Difference, became a space of both refuge and challenge for me. We grappled deeply with race; we gathered around the difficult, unmentionable topics at the center of our experiences. I became especially close with two people in that class, and our relationships became two of the first in my life where attention to how systems of power were infusing our relationships became foundational ingredients of our now years-long love and trust.

Meanwhile, in some of my other relationships, we stumbled through conversations, including ones about a course that featured a trip to occupied Palestine. Although I didn't know much about Palestine or Israel, I paid attention when Students of Color protested the class, and I began to learn. Some people I loved, though, were less willing to acknowledge the harm of visiting the settler state. A white friend of mine was enrolled in the class. Our conversations were halting, impeded by our ignorance and our conflict aversion.

In the years that followed, I continued to learn about Palestine, not by proactively studying, but because I kept encountering moments when I suddenly needed to know more—my first conflict with a family member about the Boycott, Divestment, Sanctions (BDS) of Israel movement; the first time a student of mine wanted to talk about Palestine; each spike in Israel's violence.

In 2020, after I'd spent 5 years working in schools and teaching, Colette invited me to co-facilitate HTAR. Not long after, Nama and I found ourselves on the same co-facilitation team. Almost a year later, Nama invited me to co-design HTAP. It was time to learn again.

DESCRIPTION OF THE COURSE AND RATIONALE FOR COURSE DESIGN

How to Talk About Palestine is a course on stories about Palestine. In this course, we center stories that frame Israel as a settler colony that has created structurally oppressive living conditions for Palestinians. HTAP is about encountering, critically examining, and connecting with stories that uplift lives, joys, griefs, and power dynamics in occupied Palestine.

Learning about Palestine through stories is a practice in humanization, a practice sorely lacking in mainstream media. By engaging with stories critically, we can identify the power structures that give us access to some stories and not others. We modeled our curriculum on Lee Ann Bell's *Storytelling for Social Justice* (2020), which offers a pedagogical "model for teaching about race and racism through examining the kinds of stories we tell and for developing alternative stories that account for history, power, and systemic normalizing patterns that justify inequality" (p. 1). Although Bell's work focuses on race and racism in the United States, we found the curriculum's breakdown of types of stories applicable to the Palestinian context, especially since we believe Palestine to be a racial justice issue. Through a multitude of Palestinian stories, we endeavor to support participants in their own learning and reflection, while modeling a method of teaching that they can adopt in their classrooms.

With this in mind, we designed HTAP for classroom teachers who want to talk with their students about Palestine and the Israeli occupation. We, a parent of young children and a middle-grades teacher, have encountered moments when we wanted to talk about Palestine with our children or students and found ourselves without support to do so. We want our conversations to be truthful, offer sound information, and not be solely devastating. We want them to highlight joy, possibility, and ongoing activism. Our intention is to help teacher-participants create antiracist classroom spaces where Arab (and Muslim) children feel included and all students are engaged in learning about Palestine, Palestinian liberation, and cross-struggle solidarity.

Knowing that in the current political moment talking about Palestine and Israel in schools in the United States carries risks like job loss and retaliation, we hope that the HTAP class space will become a supportive container for participants as they plan for how to teach for Palestine in their specific contexts.

CRITICAL MOMENTS OF CHALLENGES TO CREATING THIS COURSE

As we grappled with the decision to design HTAP, we realized that we had personal drives connected to it. At first, Sarah Moss was afraid of saying "yes" to a project that felt like it required a level of skill and experience she didn't feel she had. She had internalized the idea that talking about Palestine requires expertise. At the same time, Nama, a new but trusted collaborator and friend (even while hearing Sarah Moss's hesitation) was asking her to step forward. "I think we will learn a lot!" Nama said, and Sarah Moss decided it was time to take bigger risks in solidarity with Palestine. And so she said "yes."

Nama felt called to design this course, especially after experiencing another wave of institutional censorship during the 2021 Israeli attacks. Throughout the design process, she recognized that she was becoming overprotective with the course content and her stories. She needed to heal from previous dialogue efforts that dismissed and denied her lived experiences and the structural realities underpinning them. For example, Palestinian activists have criticized and rejected dialogue for normalizing ongoing injustice (Merryman-Lotze, 2018). In these dialogue programs, Palestinians and Israelis are brought together for coexistence talks and without addressing "structural and power inequalities and/or without having its goal be opposition and resistance to the Israeli occupation." Similarly oppressive dynamics sometimes exist in interfaith and intergroup dialogue efforts in the United States (see, for example, Leonardo & Porter, 2010). Working on this project together with Sarah Moss helped Nama break down her protective armor. She was willing to see if her integrity and her belonging could finally coexist together.

Now that we had decided to design HTAP, how would we do it? We decided to dream first, to give ourselves protected creative space, and to get practical later. When it felt right, we addressed our challenges head on and categorized them as follows: political contentiousness, pedagogy, and overambition.

Political Contentiousness

Talking about Palestine is hard—as is any politically contentious topic. Political contentiousness describes disagreement over narrative that makes even the framing of an issue a question of power, with real consequences. Palestinian liberation is a fraught topic in the United States, in both conservative and progressive spaces. There are concerted efforts to silence counternarratives, to make public space only for dominant narratives that justify Israel's occupation of Palestine. These narratives are plenty and shift over time. (For deeper analysis on dominant narratives, see Pappé's [2017] *Ten Myths about Israel*).

We had several conversations about potential risks in designing and teaching this course, and using our real names in this chapter. We have seen the ramifications of supporting Palestine in our communities and elsewhere—a tenured professor terminated because of a series of tweets criticizing Israel's apartheid; a school board member being pressured to resign in Fairfax County (Virginia) for supporting Palestine; and countless students and professors surveilled and added to watch lists.

Nama feels that silencing is a ploy to *hide* us, which weakens our will to act, strategize, and envision liberation; it is important for Nama to live an authentic life, and not one that caters to avoiding a watchlist. For Sarah Moss, the need for solidarity with Palestinians, as well as increasing recognition of the ways that the Israeli state promotes global militarization and state violence that impact all of us, outweighed the need to play it safe. Together, we decided that the possibilities generated in offering this course outweighed the potential risks. Possibility and collective liberation lie on the other side of risky action. And so, we envisioned a course that defies efforts to silence Palestine. The political contentiousness is still here, but we hope that our course will be a space where we can dream beyond it and prepare, as much as we can, to meet it.

Pedagogy

We addressed three main pedagogical challenges. The first was how to balance bringing in practical examples and framing while leaving ample room for reflection and discussion. For example, food is an important component in our lesson plans. Food is a site where many stories are found, shared, and passed down through generations; food is also a way for us to talk about Israel's colonial project by claiming ownership of foods like hummus and falafel. We needed to share about the politics surrounding these foods and give participants time to grapple with and dialogue about them. Without reflection and dialogue, the information stays abstract and impersonal; without the information, the dialogue is baseless. Here we are referring to two different kinds of dialogue: "dialogue" and "informed dialogue." Dialogue is a process of committed communication where participants are present to listen and hear one another to foster understanding. Informed dialogue is dialogue that explicitly acknowledges and addresses socioeconomic contexts (Zúñiga & Cytron-Walker, 2003, cited in Williams Brown, 2021).

Second, we toggled between how much to center our dialogue on *what is happening there* (in Palestine) and *what is happening here* (in the United States, to Arabs and Muslims). It was vital that we declare Palestine a racial justice issue and name the connections between the dispossession and genocide of Indigenous peoples of the so-called United States and the ways the United States and Israel depend on anti-Black and anti-Palestinian racism, respectively, to justify their actions. Many Black scholar-activists like Angela Davis and Marc Lamont Hill articulate the connections between the oppression of Black Americans and the Palestinian people. Additionally, Arab American scholars, like Nadine Naber, speak on anti-imperialism and Black–Palestinian solidarity (Naber, 2017). Both Israel and the United States employ mass incarceration, racial profiling, surveillance, and lethal force as forms of control. Operations like the "deadly exchange" are concrete examples of how Israel and the United States support each other's violence in direct ways.

Making the U.S.–Israel connection situates the struggle for Palestinian rights within the broader struggle against settler colonialism and global white supremacy. In thinking about these connections, our goal became clearer: to create a co-learning space for our participants to think through how Arab and Muslim students in the United States experience racism in schools, find ways to better support these students, and talk about connections between Palestine, Zionism, and U.S. foreign policy.

Last, we learned quickly how deeply buried counterstories about Palestine are. With that in mind, we decided that our curriculum needed to offer opportunities to practice looking for such stories as well.

Overambition

We wanted to do too much and cover too much content! We wanted to *teach* because too much is at stake to leave ambiguity, confusion, or oppressive analyses in place. We remembered our role as *facilitators:* to share analyses and stories, hold space for dialogue, and create inquiry. Our design question shifted from *What do we want our participants to know about Palestine?* to *How do we clearly frame Israel as a settler colony, dive into buried stories, art, joy, and Palestinian voices, and give ample space for participants to reflect and talk together?* In making this shift, we chose stories and activities with intention, but we also opened more fully to what our participants will bring as we guide them through their own processing and learning.

CRITICAL MOMENTS OF PROMISE THAT WE HOPE WILL COME FROM OFFERING THIS COURSE

Having not yet taught HTAP, we can only imagine its positive outcomes. However, based on our design, we believe that the course could do the following:

- Model pedagogically sound ways of engaging politically contentious topics.
- Begin conversations on how settler colonialism is foundational to Israel's occupation of Palestine.

- Help break the silence on Palestine and center it as a racial justice issue that is directly related to us in the United States.
- Nourish self-love for Arab and Muslim students by offering analyses that make sense with their life experiences and showing stories where they see themselves reflected.
- Support empathy for Palestinian experiences in non-Palestinian, non-Arab, and non-Muslim students.
- Break down efforts—sometimes simply misguided and sometimes malicious—to associate Palestinian liberation with antisemitism; these efforts dangerously misrepresent both antisemitism and Palestinian liberation.
- Support solidarity among Students of Color by clarifying the connections between Palestinian liberation, Black liberation, decolonization on Turtle Island, and all other forms of racial justice. This course also supports solidarity between white Jews and both Jewish and non-Jewish People of Color, because white supremacy is at the root of all of our oppressions.
- Be part of encouraging activism, learning, and relationship building for educators and students.
- Lead to efforts to learn, explore, and talk about other sites of American imperialism, like Afghanistan. When this window to the world is open, we can look beyond narratives of war and see countries with a deep history, rich culture, and beautiful and hospitable peoples.

Our expectation is that interest in this course will rise and fall as engagement with all racial justice topics does among the mostly white population of teachers in the United States. We hope participants will feel en-*courage*-d to teach for Palestinian liberation and know this is connected to all liberation.

LESSONS LEARNED AND RECOMMENDATIONS

For teachers and parenting adults who are ready to begin their solidarity work with Palestine, we highly recommend finding a partner to co-dream with (someone you love and trust, who is committed to antiracism, and who understands that no one is liberated if oppression exists; someone who can hold space for you when you need it, and for whom you want to do the same). Whether you are designing a course like HTAP or are looking for other ways to show up within your sphere of influence, Palestine-related content can be heavy, and pacing yourself with absorbing trauma-filled content is important.

Pedagogical Recommendations

Center joy. This does not mean we should gloss over the loss of life, but we should be mindful of how much we are teaching about pain and suffering. When you center joy, you are centering those who are alive, fighting, telling us how to support them. Centering joy means centering Palestinian voices—their creativity in resistance, their resilience in rebuilding after attacks, their needs and desires. Centering joy means centering a people, a culture, a history that is intentionally being erased. When you create a course like this and you center joy, you are resisting the status quo.

For example, we thought it important not to follow timelines that highlight popular dates and war events, like the 1967 war. Even commendable efforts that bring Palestine to the forefront often perpetuate a trope that "there is always fighting and a war going on over there," and such narratives usually create more apathy than empathy.

In centering joy, we are consciously paying attention to whom we are citing and uplifting, and where we are getting our stories and knowledge. We were intentional in bringing in knowledge and content from Palestinian and Arab scholars, many of whom have paved the way to frame Israel as a settler colonial nation. Doing so is a paradigm shift in our American thinking of Palestine and Israel. A lot can be unpacked with this framing alone: who Palestinians are and what Palestine is, how Israel came to be and the ways Zionism is conflated with Judaism, the ways we are complicit in the United States by supporting Israel with our tax dollars, and finally, the connections between the U.S. settler-colonial foundation and the ongoing genocide of Native Americans. Such a paradigm shift can encourage people into action as well as provide much needed loving support to Arab and Muslim children.

Many Ways to Support Palestine

In any type of justice-driven work there are moments of helplessness. Apartheid states, settler colonialism, illegal occupation, displacement, and global white supremacy can seem impossible to tackle. We are inundated with news bites that ask, "What is the solution? Is a two-state solution the answer?" Those answers should come from Palestinians, and many Palestinian scholars and activists have answered this question by calling for a *Free Palestine*, one that is no longer occupied by Israel. For those of us who are not Palestinians, there are many ways to show up for Palestine. To name just a few examples, actions could include signing petitions; talking about Palestine with family members; designing lesson plans that honor every child's background in the classroom; critically thinking about the ways islamophobia, racism, and antisemitism show up in schools; and boycotting items from the BDS list in your daily life. Our role is to plant the seeds, offer support and resources, and accompany our participants to their action space.

CONCLUSION

We designed HTAP to support teachers and parenting adults through conversations with children about Palestine. While witnessing the 2021 Israeli attacks, we recognized a need for support in these conversations, both in ourselves and in our broader educator communities. Children need support through moments of crisis to build understandings of the world that includes a sense of agency, and teachers and parenting adults need support for talking to children in ways that are honest while being as encouraging as possible. We hope that by sharing parts of our story, our readers will feel supported to move toward action, seek collaborators, take risks, and show up for Palestine.

REFERENCES

Bell, L. A. (2020). *Storytelling for social justice: Connecting narrative and the arts in antiracist teaching* (3rd ed.). Routledge.

Leonardo, Z., & Porter, R. K. (2010). Pedagogy of fear: Toward a Fanonian theory of "safety" in race dialogue. *Race Ethnicity and Education, 13*(10), 139–157.

Lopez, J. (2020). Healing is rhizomatic: A conceptual framework and tool. *Genealogy, 4*(4), 1–15.

Merryman-Lotze, M. (2018, March 1). When dialogue stands in the way of peace. *Friends Journal.* Accessed on January 10, 2022, from https://www.friendsjournal.org/palestine-normalization-peace.

Naber, N. (2017). "The U.S. and Israel Make the Connections for Us": Anti-Imperialism and Black-Palestinian Solidarity. *Critical Ethnic Studies, 3*(2), 15–30. http://www.jstor.org/stable/10.5749/jcritethnstud.3.2.0015.

Pappé, I. (2017). *Ten myths about Israel*. Verso.

Williams Brown, K. (2021, July 15). *IGD experience* (PowerPoint slides). Education Department, Vassar College.

Many thanks to Amre, Jennifer, Josh, Lucy, Masumi, Naadiya, and Sahara for your invaluable feedback.

CHAPTER 11

Scaling Up

The 2020 RISE for Racial Justice Public Racial Literacy Campaign and Beyond

Colette N. Cann

In June 2020, RISE for Racial Justice launched its second public racial literacy campaign, 3 years after its founding in 2017. As defined in the Introduction, a public racial literacy campaign is an intensification of effort by an organization to provide racial literacy training to the general public. This second campaign was launched in response to the increased demand for racial literacy courses by K–12 educators and parenting adults, many of whom were confused and outraged by the anti-Black racism they witnessed in spring 2020. Though anti-Black racism is a founding tool of white supremacy and the wealth that (continues to) accrues to white people in the United States, many (mostly white) educators and parenting adults were just beginning to see racism and to understand how it causes disproportionate harm to BIPOC. Without the longer historical context, the language to make sense of the differences between interpersonal and structural racism, and the tools to have difficult conversations about the murders of Black people such as George Floyd and Breonna Taylor by police, they felt at a loss for how to name what they saw on social media and how to identify a way to move forward. The increased visibility in the news of police violence against Black people, a presidential election year in the United States that centered race for political gain, and health and environmental crises that exponentially multiplied the ways that BIPOC communities were targeted by institutional and structural inequities created a need to learn about race.

As a result of its increased visibility, racism rose in the consciousness of educators and parenting adults. As they struggled to make sense of a country that would support and perpetuate racism and, as they struggled to explain racism to their students and children, they looked for help. Broadly, antiracism training organizations witnessed increases in requests for antiracism courses in spring and summer 2020 (Judkis, 2020). RISE for Racial Justice similarly experienced an increase in requests for its educator and parent racial literacy courses. Prior to 2020, we had, on average, roughly 25 requests for our introductory racial literacy course each semester. In June 2020, we had over 600 requests for our summer session.

To meet this increased need, we launched our second public racial literacy campaign. We intensified our work, increased our offerings, and built new courses. For example, in summer 2020, we offered eight sections of our introductory course, taught by 15 antiracist educators to 240 K–12 teachers and parents (we couldn't serve all 600 people who requested the course, but sent them a list of other organizations that offered similar training). Scaling up during this second campaign, though, meant attending to new details that we had previously ignored. We needed to create a sustainable model that aligned with our core principles to fairly compensate our antiracist educators, to do our work together in ways that centered racial justice and to make sure our courses were available to all regardless of ability to pay. This chapter shares our efforts to scale up and the model that resulted. I also highlight the ongoing struggles of this work.

THE NEED FOR A SECOND CAMPAIGN

At the end of our spring 2020 semester, teachers and parenting adults who had completed our introductory course, How to Talk About Racism (HTAR), asked if we might consider teaching the course again over the summer. We had never taught the course over the summer in the past because, as a team of mostly tenure-track and tenured faculty, we reserved the summer for our writing. However, in the wake of George Floyd's death on May 25th and the protests that followed, the graduates of our spring 2020 course wanted to recommend the course to their colleagues and friends.

We agreed to offer a section of the course over the summer, created an online registration form, and sent a flier for the course to our past participants to share. Then, we largely forgot about it, assuming that we would, as usual, reach about 25 participants.

However, within a day's time, we began receiving numerous emails with questions about the course; we checked the online registration form and there were literally hundreds of registered participants already. We created a waitlist for the course and, within a few weeks, over 600 people had requested the course.

The media coverage of police violence against Black people and communities put anti-Black racism on the radar of educators and parenting adults who had previously not been aware of anti-Black racism as a pandemic. This resulted in an increase in course registrations. This increase, as noted earlier, was experienced by other antiracism training organizations. However, there were other reasons for this increase.

All our courses, up through summer 2020, were offered for free. As Kim, Meredith, and I are faculty members in higher education, this work felt connected to our larger scholarship and service work, and thus we did not request compensation for this teaching. Other antiracist educators volunteered their time. As our organization is under nonprofit institutions of higher education, we also have very few costs; for example, our insurance and online platforms are provided through the institution.

And, finally, the increase in registration was related to the course being offered remotely using the Zoom platform during a time when most educators and parenting adults were sheltered in place because of the COVID-19 pandemic. Several of our participants from spring and summer 2020 talked about how important it was for them to be in community, even over Zoom, with other adults while sheltered in place. They looked forward to our time together each week because it represented a time that was set aside just for them. Additionally, with the course held remotely, participants from all over the United States (and Canada) could easily attend—there was no commute and they could take a course that was convenient by time (not location).

We want to recognize that many of our white participants noted that they had been scared to take a course on race and had been worried that they would be attacked or made to feel "bad" as a white person. The course was offered for free and so they felt that they could take a chance and drop the course with no monetary repercussions if they did not feel good in the course.

Some of our Participants of Color noted that they had been skeptical of signing up for a course on race—they didn't think they had anything to learn. Their own experience of race in the world felt sufficient. And yet they enrolled anyway, hopeful that in accompanying their white colleagues they could move the conversation about race in their schools forward. The course was free and so, other than their time and patience with their white colleagues, there was nothing to lose.

Thus, it is also important to acknowledge that "free" and "convenient" played a role in the desire to take a racial literacy course and drove the demand for our courses. This speaks to the overall reticence of our educational communities (and beyond) to engage in discussions about race. Such conversations feel terrifying for some and unnecessary for others. "Free" and "convenient" opened the door to racial literacy for many of our participants.

HOW RISE RESPONDED

With hundreds of requests for a course that only served 25, we were overwhelmed. We felt committed to providing this training; we knew well that the circumstances of the time contributed to the desire to take the course. We also felt the conspicuous limits of our capacity to respond. We were a small team who could not possibly serve all who requested the course.

We decided to attempt to scale up quickly. We reached out to our networks of antiracism trainers, friends, and colleagues with whom we had worked or whose reputation was well-known to us. We asked that they join us for summer 2020 to teach our entry-level course (HTAR) using our curriculum and pedagogy.

Once we knew how many facilitators could join us for summer 2020, we created teams of 2–3 trainers with attention to the racial and gender diversity of each team and mindful of their availability. The result was eight sections of the course. In the end, we were able to enroll over a third of those who requested the course. We put the remaining on a waitlist for fall 2020, recommended courses taught by other organizations (providing the direct link to register for those courses) and provided a list of resources for those who wanted to learn on their own.

The primary tension during this second campaign was how to provide enough freedom to the teaching teams to creatively approach their courses by drawing on their own experiences, backgrounds, and knowledges, while ensuring that participants experienced the curriculum and pedagogy of HTAR. As one of the RISE for Racial Justice co-directors, I was present on all teams except one. In my capacity as a team member across seven sections, I was able to share lessons learned and materials from one section to the next. In this way, I provided an opportunity for some consistency across course sections as well as an opportunity for shared practices. Each of the teaching teams was also provided with lesson plans for all six class sessions, a slide deck for each session (as we were teaching remotely, we used slide decks both for presentation and for engaged learning with participants), and an online Moodle site where their participants could access readings and email each other. From there, though, each team operated largely independently from each other.

We had a total of 15 facilitators for eight sections that ran Wednesdays through Sundays. Each class section met once each week for 2 hours, for a total of 6 weeks. Each teaching team met for an additional hour (at least) each week to plan. Although a detailed lesson plan for each class session had been provided, each facilitation team in the weekly planning time altered the content to reflect their own teaching style and preferences. Media used to explain concepts, for example, shifted across teams, as did the set of norms used. As I discussed in Chapter 3, what remained foundational and consistent across the sections were the use of the four levels of racism pedagogical framework, the tools for dialogue that were taught, the arc of the course (increasing risk and complexity of topics discussed overtime), and the focus on participant-centered pedagogy.

RISE for Racial Justice provided administrative support for all teams, enrolling participants in Moodle sections, building out the course modules on Moodle, and providing attendance sheets with demographic information on all participants (gender pronouns, racial identity, role identity [parenting adult, educator, etc.], and school location). RISE for Racial Justice also provided participant responses from the registration form that asked the following questions:

- How do you racially identify? What is your earliest memory of identifying racially in this way? How did you come to identify in this way? What does it mean to you to hold this racial identity?
- If a parent/guardian, how do your children racially identify themselves? (How do they think about their own racial identity? What language do they use to describe themselves? How and why do you think they came to that racial identity?)
- If a parent/guardian, how do you racially identify your children? Is it the same as how they identify themselves? Why or why not?

- Why are you interested in taking this course?
- What are some of the issues at your school related to race and racism? (This might include, but not be limited to, underrepresentation of People of Color in the curriculum and teaching staff, for example.) If you feel that your school does not have any race-related issues, please note this as well.

CONSIDERING A MOVE TO A COMPENSATION STRUCTURE

After the first few weeks of class during summer 2020, participants began to ask about how they could pay the facilitators for their work. They appreciated the effort and wanted to recognize our labor. Many noted that they appreciated the personal attention they received in the course and that they were surprised that they had such access to the instructors to ask questions and to get feedback on their written homework.

However, we had no compensation model in place. As an organization that offered courses for free, we did not even have a *way* to accept payment from participants. In an email discussion with the summer facilitators, it was decided that we would identify two organizations that addressed anti-Black racism and anti-immigration attacks in education and ask that participants donate money to these organizations on behalf of our class community.

The first organization that we selected is Making Us Matter, an online extracurricular school for middle and high school students. Making Us Matter focuses on making the lives of Black people matter in curricula, pedagogy, and staffing. We asked participants to donate to the school through the school's online campaign (https://givebutter .com/hellablack). Though it was difficult to track all the donations that came from our participants (donations can be made anonymously without revealing the amount donated), we were able to identify at least $6,000 in donations. In addition, there were over $2,000 in donations that were received in the same time period anonymously in the amount we recommended for donation.

The second fund that we selected is the Que Llueva Café scholarship for undocumented high school students. For over a decade, this scholarship fund has provided $500 grants to graduating undocumented high school students to provide additional financial support for the first year of college. Sixteen participants from our summer 2020 courses donated $25–$300 each to this organization, for a total of $1,653.

At summer's end, most of the course facilitators moved onto other work. One went to graduate school; three returned to community organizing, nonprofit work, and consulting; and four returned to administrative positions in higher education. It was understood that they had partnered with us to get us through the unexpected uptick in requests for HTAR, but that they would not be able to facilitate with us long term. Eight of us, though, continued into the following academic year. With the new larger team, we decided that this was a time to pause to consider whether our prior model, offering free courses, was supportive of other organizations doing similar work, communicated the importance of antiracism training, and sustainably supported the well-being of our facilitators. We held a remote retreat to discuss how to proceed.

At the retreat, several facilitators argued that offering our courses for free or "donate at will" undermined other organizations that do this same work and rely on the income to continue to do their work. Participants, hesitant to take an antiracism course, would likely select a free course over a paid course from another organization. It was important to us that we not undermine (or compete with) other organizations that offer antiracism training. We see our work as aligning with the work of other racial literacy organizations and believe our efforts should be collective.

Others at the retreat noted that offering a course for free communicates that the labor of our facilitators is not valued and that the content of the course is somehow optional in the lives and work of educators and those parenting.

What and how our participants learn about race in our courses offers them something inherently valuable: the opportunity to reflect on how they were socialized and conditioned to participate in and reproduce racism and white supremacy in their worlds and begin the long, slow, and oftentimes painful process of unlearning racism. They learn that they can talk about race and how to talk about race, and begin to envision how they can take antiracist action. Menakem (2017) refers to this as an opportunity to process "clean pain"—"pain that mends and can build [our] capacity for growth" (p. 19). Taking a course on race, racism, and antiracism can offer participants a chance to begin a life-long journey to create anti-oppressive schooling spaces for young people.

And, finally, we wanted to rethink our structure to recognize that our facilitators have very real material needs. Especially during a global pandemic, when at least one person had lost a job and several others had increased monetary needs, we wanted to be able to support them in any way possible. While they are dedicated to this work and would (and did) facilitate without compensation, they should not have to. And, as more than half of the facilitators identify as BIPOC and at least half of our participants in some of the courses identify as white, we felt deeply uncomfortable about the dynamics in place when the course was offered for free. We had to find our way to an acceptance and acknowledgement that being compensated for antiracism training is not exploitative of this historical moment. No facilitator is becoming oppressively wealthy through this work.

DEVELOPING A TRANSPARENT STRUCTURAL MODEL

The Roots

What resulted is a structure that needs ongoing work and rethinking. It is not perfect by any means. Yet we share it, in all of its imperfection, because we recognize that this side of the work is often invisible. Our model is rooted in three critical approaches to collective antiracism work: Rhonda Magee's Foundations for Racial Justice, the Black Lives Matter principles, and Community Care Values.

Magee (2019), in her seminal text, *The Inner Work of Racial Justice*, identifies core "attitudes or traits," grounded in a tradition of mindfulness, that support internal and interpersonal antiracism work. She refers to these as the "foundations for racial justice work" (p. 31). These include the following attitudes necessary to do this reflective self-work and work with others:

1. An "openness to explore without judgment"
2. A willingness to show "care and concern for the well-being" of ourselves and each other
3. A willingness to "act to alleviate the suffering" of those within and outside of our community
4. The pursuit of a patience with ourselves, with others, and with the process of racial awareness and racial justice
5. A willingness to embrace the "don't know" mind, to "accept our own ongoing need to learn, and to live with the inevitable uncertainty"
6. A willingness to stay the course toward racial justice even through "setbacks," inevitable failure, and impatience with the slow process
7. The "courage to seek and act for justice" (pp. 31–33)

These seven foundations not only guide us in our work with each other as a team of facilitators and the work we do with participants, but also inform how we go about caring for each other and our participants in this work. For example, an important part of caring for each and our community of participants is to be mindful of our material needs, putting that "care and concern" above profit, while also being mindful to pay a fair honorarium to our facilitators.

Our model is also built on the articulated principles of the global Black Lives Matter network and the localized Black Lives Matter at School 13 Guiding Principles (D.C. Area Educators for Social Justice, n.d.), which emphasizes that the process of getting free is as important as the outcome to be free. How we treat each other as we do racial justice work must also be just, loving, and kind. We center intersectional justice in our practice with each other and in our courses, acknowledge and fight against anti-Black racism (and settler colonialism) specifically, and make our spaces family friendly (especially as so many of our facilitators and participants parented from home during the COVID-19 pandemic).

And, finally, our work is based on Community Care Values as designed by Shift Consulting (https://www.shiftingculture.co). Community Care Values decenter white supremacist culture in our work together—that is, decentering individualism, perfectionism, and power hoarding, for example, as ways of doing work established by systems of racial oppression. Community Care Values recenter values such as "normalizing failure," "moving at the speed of trust," "collectivism," "an abundance mindset," and "centering and reimagining rest" (Shift Consulting, 2020). In embracing an "abundance mindset," for example, we approach our work knowing that our needs will be met when we do our work with integrity and community. We "move at the speed of trust" rather than at a speed motivated by generating ever-increasing profit, and we honor our colleagues who need to move back from the work in order to prioritize their own wellness. This includes our participants; we provide refunds without question to those who realize that they do not have time to take a class.

To be transparent, we did not sit as a group and identify the foundations for our work together prior to developing our tuition and compensation model. We were not linear about this process. It was messy at best. Yet our work, even without articulating it as such, was informed by these three approaches described above. They inform the norms that we use in our courses, and we draw on them in our everyday lives. In our clearest conversations, when we asked ourselves what we really wanted to achieve through this tuition and compensation model, our conversations took us back to values and principles articulated in all three.

The Learning Process

We also did quite a bit of self-education around how to set up a model that works best for us. Through an organization called SCORE, we took several courses in budgeting, payroll, and advertising and growing a business. SCORE is "a nonprofit organization . . . dedicated to helping small businesses get off the ground, grow and achieve their goals through education and mentorship" (SCORE, 2021). Their courses are offered for, on average, $25 per class and taught in the remote environment.

Additionally, SCORE offers free mentorship. We signed up for the mentorship program and, with our assigned mentor, explored different models for our tuition and compensation structure. You are allowed to select your mentor from a list that highlights mentors' backgrounds and areas of expertise. We selected someone who taught the courses we had attended as we already knew him to be supportive of centering the mission of the organization in the work. As well, he communicated humility and embraced the "don't know mind" (Magee, 2019); he never hesitated to acknowledge what he did not know.

In our work with our mentor, he started by acknowledging that he did not know much about academia and education, but that he could support us by asking questions and referring us to resources. And true to his word, at every turn, he reminded us that we need not use a "traditional business model"; though we were guided by principles that were anti-profit, we found ourselves occasionally getting swept up in the moment. Our coach, as any good coach does, continued to remind us that our tuition and compensation structure should align with who we are as an organization and our mission. In many ways, he noted, we are trying to do something different.

He also reduced some of the fear that we had in designing a tuition and compensation model. As academics, none of the co-directors were trained in accounting and managing money for small businesses (though we now believe a good money management course would be useful in every school of education). He helped us think through whether we needed business insurance, whether we needed to hire an external payroll company, and whether to secure the services of a lawyer. The resulting model is as follows.

First, all incoming monies and expenses (materials and payments to facilitators) are transparently shared on a spreadsheet. All facilitators who facilitate with us (even if they take a sabbatical semester) have access to this shared spreadsheet. *Everyone* knows how much money each course generates and how much each facilitator and administrator is paid.

Importantly, all facilitators are paid the same. Some of our courses generate no income; we remain committed to offering free courses to educators and parenting adults at public schools that have no budgets for this work. Our introductory level course generates roughly $6,000 per course, while our intermediate courses and advanced course (offered for career facilitators and university faculty) can generate over $20,000. Regardless of whether a facilitator teaches a free course to a public school or the advanced course, each facilitator makes $1,700 per course. Additionally, all facilitators can take courses offered within our organization tuition-free.

We also offer scholarships to participants. Rather than asking them to prove to us that they need a scholarship, we only ask what they can afford to pay at the time. We provide the opportunity for them to pay over time if they like. And, finally, we give them the opportunity to pay when they can; participants are welcome to enroll in the course and pay years later in the form of a donation. We found, especially during the pandemic, that participants experienced a lot of shame around money. The conversations about scholarships were challenging for them. We reiterated, time and again, that they needed only identify how much they could pay at the time and we would do our best to honor that.

Though not a part of our model, we also want to highlight here the work of the Anti-Oppressive Resource and Training Alliance (AORTA; see http://aorta.coop). They offer a level of transparency to which we aspire. First, they make visible on their website where the tuition from participants goes (AORTA, n.d.), noting the percentage that goes toward salaries, benefits, operating expenses, and for additional costs (such as payments to independent contractors). The bulk of the tuition (80%) goes toward salaries and benefits.

They account for structural and institutional racism in their payment structure by asking participants to select the amount they pay for each course—the amount they pay is related to their inherited wealth and wealth accumulated through historically racist policies as well as their work status.

CONCLUSION

We want to acknowledge that institutional affiliation and the privileges that accompany that affiliation allow us to pursue a model that does not prioritize profit. Our organization sits under the umbrella of a university; thus, we have few overhead costs. A university processes our tuition and honoraria to facilitators, offers us access to the software and platforms that we use (such as Zoom and Google Suite), and provides affiliated nonprofit status so that we can host our website and other memberships (such as our membership with our management tool, Base Camp, and course Moodle sites) at the nonprofit rate. We are also insured under the affiliation with the university.

Hands down, our least favorite part of this journey has been setting up the tuition and compensation model. Just *talking* about money feels bad. Accepting payment feels bad. In fact, the first semester that we were able to compensate facilitators, half of them refused the payment or asked for the payment to be donated to a nonprofit. It was important to us, though, to include this chapter on our developing tuition and compensation model to open the conversation in a public space and invite others into the discomfort to see what we, collectively, might envision as alternatives to our society's addiction to exploitative models of business.

REFERENCES

AORTA. (n.d.). *Rates*. Retrieved March 27, 2022, from http://aorta.coop/rates.

D.C. Area Educators for Social Justice. (n.d.). *13 guiding principles*. Retrieved March 27, 2022, from https://www.dcareaeducators4socialjustice.org/black-lives-matter/13-guiding-principles.

Judkis, M. (2020, July 8). Anti-racism trainers were ready for this moment. Is everyone else? *Washington Post*. Retrieved January 10, 2022, from https://www.washingtonpost.com/lifestyle/style/anti-racism-trainers-were-ready-for-this-moment-is-everyone-else/2020/07/07/df2d39ea-b582-11ea-a510-55bf26485c93_story.html.

Magee, R. (2019). *The inner work of racial justice: Healing ourselves and transforming our communities through mindfulness*. TarcherPerigee.

Menakem, R. (2017). *My grandmother's hands: Racialized trauma and the pathway to mending our hearts and bodies*. Central Recovery Press.

SCORE. (2021, July 29). *Mission, vision and values. Homepage*. Retrieved March 27, 2022, from https://www.score.org/content/mission-vision-and-values.

Shift Consulting. (2020, October). *Speakout youth summit* (webinar).

Closing

Within these pages, our hope was to humanize our work and our team members. Too often, the messiness and uncertainty of social justice efforts are sanitized and put on a pedestal as exemplars. Certainly, we need those examples. So, too, though, do we need to see behind the curtains; we need access to the internal dialogue filled with uncertainty, worries, and history of changes made and new paths taken in our work.

In every moment in the book, between every page, we hope that readers found humility as we sought to highlight the challenges of this work. Oftentimes, books such as this make the process look neat—almost easy. This work is complex and difficult, and many nights we lose sleep over stories that were shared, classes during which we struggled as facilitators, and worries about alternative paths we might have taken.

We also hope you have felt the love that emanates from the facilitator communities we have been able to create doing this work. Antiracist work must happen in community, and doing it with the talented, brilliant facilitators you have met through this book, as well as the other facilitators not included here, have all informed and enhanced our practice significantly. We are grateful for this community. It keeps us going in the challenging moments and reminds us that we are not alone.

And, finally, this book has served as an opportunity for reflection and yet another reason for the RISE for Racial Justice community to gather and rethink what we do and how we do it. What we capture in print today is only a springboard to new ways to teach tomorrow.

In solidarity,
Colette, Kim, and Meredith

Afterword

"A Racially Literate Mobilization"
Advancing Collective Racial Literacy
in Education

Riverside Unified School District (RUSD) is situated on the land of the Cahuilla, Luiseño, and Tongva people, who are the original stewards and continue to advocate for the well-being of the earth and their people. In October 2021, a Native student filmed Candice Reed—a white teacher in RUSD—teaching a math lesson while mocking Indigenous culture. As the video went viral, local Indigenous communities organized to hold the school accountable to recognize and repair the harm. The teacher was eventually fired; however, it came to light that she had been teaching this lesson for years, enacting harmful representations of Native people throughout her professional tenure. One local Indigenous protester lamented, "she has instilled stereotypes and misinformation to a whole generation of students" (Shin, 2022).

Layered upon systemic racism such as resource inequities and a Eurocentric curriculum, U.S. schools are fraught with practices, people, and moments that perpetuate racial harm. Unfortunately, Candice Reed is not an anomaly, but rather is joined by numerous K–12 educators who lack the racial literacy needed to engage in respectful, humanizing ways with the growing number of Black, Indigenous, and People of Color students that make up over half the U.S. public-school population. From the white teacher in North Carolina who told her Black students that without the constitution, they would be her field slaves; to the white teacher in New York State who held a mock slave auction; to the group of white teachers in Idaho that dressed up for a team building activity as the United States–Mexico wall, we see countless examples of educators who do not have the needed understanding of historical and contemporary structural racism.

In my professional role as a teacher educator and researcher of teaching and teacher preparation, the questions I continue to get asked when people hear of these incidents are, "Who trained these teachers?" "Why were they allowed to be teachers?" The reality is our teaching force has been and continues to be overwhelmingly white, monolingual, and race-evasive. And teacher education is complicit in the reproduction of whiteness in the teaching force. Today 70% of teacher candidates (AACTE, 2019), 87% of adjunct instructors, and 91% of tenured/tenure track instructors are white (King & Hampel, 2018). Souto-Manning (2019) argues that programs operate through "White ways and systems of knowing" (p. 100), avoiding racial discourse and maintaining white comfort (Kohli et al., 2021). Once teachers enter the workforce, school-based teacher professional development similarly avoids overt and candid discourse on race (Kohli, 2022). So where are teachers getting the tools they need to challenge racism? And relatedly, how can teachers support students to navigate a world fraught with racism if they do not even understand how to identify it themselves, let alone are perpetuating it?

If we truly desire a society equipped to redress racism and advance racial justice, a 21st-century education must be defined beyond technology and common core—there must be a collective racial literacy to the past and current harm that Communities of Color endure. In 2004, the late Harvard law professor Lani Guinier echoed critical race scholar Derrick Bell's lamentation on the shortcomings of *Brown v. Board of Education of Topeka* (1954), arguing that racial progress cannot come from the courts alone. She called for "a racially literate mobilization of people within and across lines of race, class, and geography" (p. 118) who carry "the ability to read race in conjunction with both contemporary institutional and democratic hierarchies and their historical antecedents." She called for a racial literacy embodied by diverse stakeholders.

In my own work, which is dedicated to diversifying the teaching force and strengthening the racial literacies of teachers, I have met many K–12 educators who fight tirelessly against racism to build something different, to create spaces where students are seen, cared for, and valued. Consider the teacher in Oʻahu who weaves Native Hawaiian cultural practices into her 5th-grade classroom so students *and* their parents can relearn the community knowledge that, she argues, is evaporating in schools, and the teacher in the Central Valley, CA, who fought alongside multiracial community organizations for Ethnic Studies classes that teach the resistance histories of their people so students understand their agency in the face of power and injustice (Kohli, 2021). These re-imaginations of teaching are possible when teachers have racial literacies and understand the imperative to challenge institutionalized policies and practices. Only if teachers, administrators, and various educational stakeholders understand the racialized realities of Students of Color, their families, and communities, can they engage in and/or stand in solidarity with them in this work.

At a time with much national opposition to race discourse in schools, with rampant attempts to ban racialized historical content and literature, this book is a beautiful reflection and road map to interrupting racial harm and supporting the growth of educators who are equipped to identify and disrupt racism. I commend the authors who dreamed and built beautiful community courses for educators, parents, and youth to support their sense-making of racialization in schools and society. Contextualized in the long history of Communities of Color and community organizations fighting for and building racial literacy education, this book is a timely and powerful contribution, showing us a way forward on the path toward racial justice.

—Rita Kohli, PhD

REFERENCES

AACTE (American Association of Colleges for Teacher Education). (2019). *Education students and diversity: A national portrait.*

Guinier, L. (2004). From racial liberalism to racial literacy: *Brown v. Board of Education* and the interest-divergence dilemma. *Journal of American History, 91*(1), 92–118.

King, J., & Hampel, R. (2018). *Colleges of education: A national portrait.* AACTE.

Kohli, R., Dover. A., Jayakumar, U., Lee, D., Henning, N., Comeaux, E., Nevárez, A., Hipolito, E., Carreno Cortez, A., & Vizcarra, M. (2021). Towards a healthy racial climate in teacher education: Centering the well-being of teacher candidates of color. *Journal of Teacher Education*, 1–14.

Shin, T. (2022). Riverside teacher fired months after video shows her dancing in mock Native American headdress. https://www.nbclosangeles.com/news/local/riverside-teacher-fired-video-sohcahtoa-headdress-native-american/2817486/.

Souto-Manning, M. (2019). Toward praxically-just transformations: Interrupting racism in teacher education. *Journal of Education for Teaching, 1*(45), 97–113. https://doi.org/10.1080/02607476.2019.1550608.

About the Authors
and the Contributors

Brett Collins (she/her) is a social worker, educator, and mother who grew up on occupied Ohlone land, also known as San Francisco, CA. She most often racialized as white but also identifies as being a Gringa Latina. She has been a facilitator with RISE for Racial Justice for 1.5 years and had the joy of co-creating the HTAR Community of Reflective Practice (CORP) with Masumi Hayashi-Smith. She owes the major milestones in her formal antiracism journey to Drs. Colette Cann, Allison Briscoe-Smith, and Jessica Daniel. In addition, she gives thanks to her mentor clinicians, Dawn Belkin-Martinez and Dr. Joanna Herrera, for instilling in her the tools of narrative therapy and reflective practice. Now, as a therapist, consultant, and faculty lecturer at San Francisco State University, she calls on the wisdom and steadfastness of these womxn to advocate for equity and liberation in early education and beyond. Further credit goes to the children, families, and comrades that educated her about power and privilege in "the real world." Her relationships within child welfare, mental health, and juvenile "justice" systems taught her that abolitionism takes many forms but always starts with herself.

Colette N. Cann (she/they) is an activist-scholar Mother of Color who currently serves as a professor and a co-associate dean in the School of Education at the University of San Francisco. Colette is a co-founder of RISE for Racial Justice and currently serves as its director. Her scholarship has allowed her to collaborate with teachers, students, and community organizations and has appeared in journals such as *Race, Ethnicity and Education, Whiteness and Education, Urban Education, Journal of Peace Education, Qualitative Inquiry*, and *Cultural Studies <–> Critical Methodologies*. Her most recent publication is the co-authored book *The Activist Academic: Engaged Scholarship for Resistance, Hope and Social Change*. She earned her BA from Stanford University and completed both her MA and PhD at the Graduate School of Education at UC Berkeley.

Kimberly Williams Brown (she/her) is the co-founder and director of the Intergroup Dialogue Collective, a nonprofit that uses intergroup dialogue praxis to engage in critical conversations about race and racism. She is an assistant professor at Vassar College in Education, Africana Studies, and Women's Studies. She holds a PhD and a certificate of Advanced Study from Syracuse University in Cultural Foundations of Education and Women and Gender Studies. Her scholarship sits at the intersection of race, gender, and migration. She is published in *The Oxford Handbook for Educational Research*; *Women's Study Anthology*; *American Indian Cultural and Research Journal* (AICRJ); and the *Handbook of Teachers of Color and Indigenous Teachers* through the American Educational Research Association (AERA).

Masumi Hayashi-Smith (they/she) is a biracial facilitator and music teacher originally from Coast Salish land in Tacoma, WA. With training in Kodaly pedagogy (M.M.), Orff Schulwerk, and Waldorf approaches to music teaching, Masumi is active in conversations around conscientious use of materials, culturally responsive teaching, and relationships with culture bearers. In undergraduate study, Masumi concentrated in Africana Studies, and then, with a Fulbright fellowship, researched the political aspects of history education in post-war Sri Lanka. Currently, Masumi teaches with RISE for Racial Justice, Intergroup Dialogue Collective, Holy Names University, and Alma Partners. They are also a music director for Thrive Choir.

Meredith Madden (she/her) is a mother, activist-scholar, and decolonial feminist pedagogue. She is the founder and director of The Equity Prof, where she provides educators with professional development in antiracism and social justice for the purpose of creating spaces of inclusion, belonging, equity, and justice in education. She is an assistant professor of education at Utica University. She also facilitates on intergroup dialogue pedagogy for RISE for Racial Justice. Meredith holds a PhD in Cultural Foundations of Education and a Certificate of Advanced Study in Women's and Gender Studies from Syracuse University.

She also holds an MS in Urban Education (Mercy College), and a Master of Public Policy with a social policy concentration (the George Washington University). She completed the University of

Pennsylvania's Penn Equity Institute on Race and Equity and is a trained intergroup dialogue facilitator. She proudly began her social consciousness-raising in the sociology classrooms of her undergraduate alma mater, Hobart and William Smith Colleges. Her research can be found in *Equity and Excellence in Education* and *Feminist Teacher.*

Nama Khalil (she/hers) is faculty at Columbus College of Art and Design where she teaches Introduction to Anthropology and Media Anthropology. She received her PhD in Sociocultural Anthropology from the University of Michigan. Nama's work highlights the intersections of expressive culture and social justice, specifically the ways young people use alternative media and storytelling to impact social change. She directed *Hijabi Monologues* (2013) and curated *Another Way of Looking: Influences from Islam* (2009) and *Creative Dissent: Art of Arab World Uprisings* (2013). Her art and writing have appeared in MOMA's Design and Violence exhibition, Designo14, and OWPAL's QuaranZine. Outside of academia, she does antiracism training for educators and community organizations. She was a 2021 fellow with the Muslim Anti-Racism Collaborative and has been a facilitator with RISE for Racial Justice since 2020.

Robin Mallison Alpern (she/her) is a white cisgender woman raised in the Religious Society of Friends (Quakers). She has had a lifelong concern for racial justice and equity. She works with antiracism organizations in her home community and among Quakers, including cross-racial groups and white caucus groups. Her antiracist vision and practice have been informed and shaped by a multitude of mentors and leaders, both white and of color. As Director of Training at the Center for the Study of White American Culture (CSWAC), Robin co-designed and co-leads a series of workshops on "What White People Can Do About Racism." She co-facilitates a dedicated group on "Raising Anti-Racist Children" at CSWAC's online organizing platform, the Anti-Racist Community Network. Robin's focus is on engaging white people in work for racial justice and equity. She teaches white people about internalized patterns of racial superiority and complicity in white supremacy, both historically and in current times. Robin has raised four antiracist white children who teach her every day how to make the world a better place.

Sade Ojuola (she/her) is a DEI practitioner and educator from Oakland, CA, with experience spanning K–12, higher education, and both the nonprofit and tech sectors. She is passionate about examining the experiences of BIPOC, navigating predominantly white educational and professional spaces, as well as creating an affirming environment for all marginalized groups within them. As a product of such spaces, her own experiences have been a catalyst for her work and research. Sade has a master's in International and Multicultural Education from the University of San Francisco, where she gained a deep appreciation for critical race theory as a lens that uniquely explicates and illuminates the truth of America's racial past and present. Previously, she worked as the Assistant Director of Admissions at the Nueva School. Today, she is the Diversity, Inclusion, and Belonging Coordinator at Reddit. She is also a mindfulness instructor, firmly believing that anti-racism work and mindfulness practices go hand in hand.

Sarah Moss Yanuck (she, ze) is a white, queer, Ashkenazi Jew who was raised on the lands of the Skarure/Tuscarora, Shakori, Saponi, Occaneechi, Lumbee, and Eno peoples (colonially known as Chapel Hill and Durham, NC) among oak trees, roly-polies, and red clay dirt. She is, among other things, a granddaughter, a daughter, a sister, a lover of stories, a K–12 teacher, a facilitator, and a songleader. Ze has been teaching and working in schools since 2015, facilitating with RISE for Racial Justice since summer 2020, and facilitating with the Intergroup Dialogue Collective since February 2021. She is sustained in this work by collaborative friendships and their facilitation-nerd-out phone calls, which become fertile ground for creativity, clarity, and connection. She currently lives in Lenapehoking in West Philadelphia. According to her 6th-grade students, Sarah Moss sings frequently and always wears warm sweaters.

T. Gertrude Jenkins (she/they) is a 15-year educator, specializing in grades 9–12 Language Arts. Over the course of her career, she has taught in Orlando, FL; Atlanta, GA; and Redwood City, CA. Jenkins is currently pursuing a doctorate at the University of San Francisco as part of the International and Multicultural Education program in the School of Education. Her research focuses on the experiences of Black teachers against the backdrop of anti-Blackness in K–12 school systems. As a co-founder of Making Us Matter, an education activism nonprofit, Jenkins works to provide an education space that rejects whiteness as the standard for academic achievement. Her work is motivated by her desire to provide alternative options for schooling that are free of the many systemic messages of anti-Blackness that are constantly transmitted in our current school systems.

Index